SUMMIT ROUNDUP

Profiles of 21 World Leaders

SUMMIT ROUNDUP

Profiles of 21 World Leaders

by

WILLIAM H. STRINGER

With sixteen photographs by
GORDON N. CONVERSE

LONGMANS, GREEN AND COMPANY
NEW YORK · LONDON · TORONTO
1959

LONGMANS, GREEN AND CO., INC.
119 WEST 40TH STREET, NEW YORK 18

LONGMANS, GREEN AND CO., LTD.
6 & 7 CLIFFORD STREET, LONDON W 1

LONGMANS, GREEN AND CO.
20 CRANFIELD ROAD, TORONTO 16

SUMMIT ROUNDUP: PROFILES OF 21 WORLD LEADERS

PUBLISHED SIMULTANEOUSLY IN THE DOMINION OF CANADA BY
LONGMANS, GREEN AND CO., TORONTO

FIRST EDITION

LIBRARY OF CONGRESS CATALOG CARD NUMBER 59–14399

Printed in the United States of America

To

“Gx”

Contents

Illustrations

Introduction

THE TRULY authentic Summit Conference—which can dispel international prejudice and suspicion—must be convened in the hearts and minds of men.

The agenda calls for a people-to-people, nation-to-nation, prime minister-to-president understanding of each other's vast problems, honest endeavors, and high aspirations.

This book is an attempt to convene that kind of Summit Conference in the heart of the reader. It is an effort to provide a constructive, helpful picture of the key leaders of planet earth, and the peoples they serve—to see sympathetically what they are trying to accomplish, often against overwhelming odds—to look beyond the spot-news headlines.

When I began this 30,000 mile globe-girdling assignment, in which I would visit twenty-five countries, travel on twenty-four airlines and profile twenty-one world leaders, I wondered how mankind would add up. Would I find thoughtful awareness of humanity's common lot? Would I discover earnest hopes to win favorable notice in the annals of history? Would there be boastfulness or the braggadocio that comes from fear? Would there be mysticism and unalertness? Would I find handsome achievements, here and there, to lift fellow beings into living standards and opportunities worthy of the twentieth century?

I must affirm that not a single president or prime minister proved to be unattractive or without merit. Each individual—Nehru, Nasser, Ben-Gurion, Adenauer, Sukarno, and the rest—loomed as patriotic according to his own lights. All were surprisingly human, none were bombastic or strutting, though obviously a few faults were visible around the fringes of virtue.

And the people themselves! How diverse in custom, yet how similar in humanity they seemed, when viewed close up, spoken to, talked with. There were, of course, vast inequalities of opportunity, widely varying environments, and occasionally some dangerous indoctrinations. But when one considers the people as individuals—the Filipino taxi driver, the guide at the Indian dam, the Japanese farmer, the waiter at Zagreb, the Bombay matron, the member of the London cast of *My Fair Lady*—people yellow, brown, black, or white are, way down deep, not so vastly unlike one another, anywhere on this globe.

When *The Christian Science Monitor*'s chief photographer, Mr. Gordon Converse, and I began our safari, it was decided to select the twenty-one presidents and prime ministers on the basis of personal achievement, world renown, power wielded, and geographical balance. In a tight schedule, some leader might be unavailable or traveling abroad. Three proved elusive, but in each such case a profile was written on the spot, drawing on reliable and intimate sources.

In each interview I put two basic questions to the president or prime minister:

1. What is your country's essential, individual role in world affairs, as you visualize it?

2. What, to you, is the most encouraging or exciting domestic development now under way in your land?

Responses derived from such a polyglot cross section of international leadership were revealing. Here indeed was interdependence. Here were aspirations surprisingly similar. But almost every leader staked out a highly individualistic role and destiny for his country in foreign affairs. There is no drab sameness among the kingdoms of earth.

If only each of us—whether we wear a gray flannel suit, an Indian sari, or a robe of African *kente* cloth—could realize how true it is that we inhabitants of earth are "all in the same boat," with such a deal of unfinished business to attend to.

There is pertinence in the pithy comment made by General Charles de Gaulle to his first press conference as president of France:

"When two-thirds of the inhabitants of earth lead a miserable existence while certain peoples have at their disposal what is necessary to assure the progress of all, is this the time for the dangerous fuss over West Berlin?"

Of course West Berlin and every bastion of freedom must be defended! But neither the Communists nor our own fears should be permitted totally to monopolize our thinking with rumors of war and nuclear holocaust. How useful occasionally to look about us and see with wider perception the struggles and upward-strivings of mankind's diverse races!

I would add a final point. The day of the rough-talking, sensation-seeking journalist is about over in Asia and Africa. These people want thoughtful, understanding reporting. This doesn't mean glossing over faults and failures. It does mean balance, correct analysis, and no condescension, open or subtle. I nearly lost one major interview because of the dispatches of a Western journalist who preceded me. People in the newly emergent countries carry chips on their shoulders. But kindness wins their hearts.

I am grateful to the Board of Trustees of The Christian Science Publishing Society for permission to reprint the "Summit Interviews" from the *Monitor* on which this book is based.

To my *Monitor* colleagues all around the globe who contributed so helpfully to this venture, and in particular to Erwin D. Canham, Saville R. Davis, and Joseph G. Harrison, I am deeply grateful, as I am to Mr. Converse, the unfailing "good companion" of one hundred days of rapid transit. Deepest thanks go also to my wife for her intuitive assistance in dispatching useful news clippings to me in far-off lands.

William H. Stringer

Washington, D.C.
June, 1959

SUMMIT ROUNDUP

Profiles of 21 World Leaders

1

Eisenhower

(U.S.A.)

Washington

WORLD EVENTS—and Moscow's continued "probing, probing, probing"—have conspired to keep Dwight D. Eisenhower from being the kind of American president he would most like to be.

Soviet Premier Nikita S. Khrushchev's Berlin challenge is a case in point, though it also presents Mr. Eisenhower with the opportunity of going down in history as the one who led his country through its most hazardous crisis since Korea.

But over the long pull—as through the crises of Quemoy, Indo-China, Berlin, and all the rest—what particularly troubles President Eisenhower is that, because the cold war continues (with occasional hotter exchanges) and because heavy armanent expenditures are a constant necessity, the United States is prevented from doing many of the constructive things it could otherwise accomplish, abroad as well as at home.

When, indeed, the question is put to the powerful president of the United States: "What, in your opinion, is or should be your country's essential and special role in today's world?" he would prefer to answer in words to this effect:

"The United States should be leading the world up those exciting new paths of joint action in probing outer space, developing nuclear power, conquering pestilence, expanding the frontiers of science."

Instead, the dire necessities of self-preservation and preparedness in the face of aggression require that he answer in this wise:

"The United States must untiringly concentrate on keeping itself strong, on maintaining common purpose with its essential allies, on assisting nonaligned nations to be sturdily independent. It must be alert to forestall encroachments on freedom anywhere in the world."

This is not to suggest—nor would the president suggest—that the United States must be so engrossed with the East-West power struggle that Washington has no time to take the lead in constructive measures to lessen tension and instill cooperation.

But there are questions of finances and the budget. There are only so many hours in the day. Berlin is an insistent alarm. And Mr. Eisenhower is breaking in a new foreign-policy chief. He cannot tackle everything as he would like to.

Nor is it suggested that the president was reluctant in assuming larger leadership in the Berlin crisis. Associates have remarked that, despite the leaving of the once-indispensable presidential assistant Sherman Adams and the absence, through sickness, of Secretary of State John Foster Dulles, Mr. Eisenhower was in particularly good spirits. He held a record nine press conferences in a row. He conferred more frequently with individual Cabinet members and top members of Congress, who were no longer barred from his door by the frosty "no" of protective Chief of Staff Adams.

"Whenever there is a major challenge, a complex world issue, which appeals to his combative temper, the president rises to it. I've seen this time and again," declared a White House official who works intimately with Mr. Eisenhower.

This was on a Saturday at 9 A.M. and this official was temporarily handling appointments and admissions at the president's door. Secretary of State Christian A. Herter had just been in to discuss policy with the president.

Mrs. Anne Whitman, the president's secretary, appeared briefly from the inner sanctum. "No interruptions now, he says," she commanded. The president was working on a new "speech to the nation." Malcolm Moos of Johns Hopkins, speech-writing assistant at the White House, was to be the only consultant admitted.

"The president is taking on more of the drawing together, the working up, of policy—as well as making the final policy decisions themselves," this official explained.

Like a seasoned fire horse, the president seems to enjoy a call to action.

Yet his feeling that there is so much else that the world could and should be doing, that mankind could devote its energies to purposes so much wiser, crops out continually here and there, even in his press-conference comments. As when he recently remarked:

"On the other side of the picture, we are not living the kind of normal—what we'd like to call a normal—life of thinking more of our own affairs, of thinking of the education and happiness of our children, and all that sort of thing which should occupy our minds . . . we are living in a sort of half world."

Back in 1954, in a prepared address at Christmastime, the president stated his thoughts more succinctly in these words: "With those who stand against us, in fear or in ignorance of our intentions, we have chosen the hard way of patient, tireless search in every avenue that may lead to their better understanding of our peaceful purposes. They know, as well as we, that the world is large enough, the skills of man great enough, to feed and to clothe and to house mankind in peace.

"This universal knowledge can be the fruitful beginning of prosperous life together."

Interestingly enough, Mr. Khrushchev has similarly alluded to the great strides which humanity could accomplish if wars and suspicions could be laid aside. But he has not matched deeds to his words, in Washington's view.

What does the president have particularly in mind when he alludes to constructive pursuits?

The International Geophysical Year is an excellent example of nations working together, he points out. The IGY projects helped greatly to expand man's knowledge of his material environment—of Antarctic regions, of astronomical behavior, of the tides and forces and weather of planet earth.

Most of us recall the verve which Mr. Eisenhower put into his appearance at the United Nations in December, 1953, when he launched the "atoms for peace" proposal, declaring: "The United States pledges . . . to devote its entire heart and mind to find the way by which the miraculous inventiveness of man shall not be dedicated to his death, but consecrated to his life."

At the United Nations he was being the kind of president he particularly likes to be.

But the international atomic energy agency at Vienna, the child of his proposal, has not been able to accomplish very much so far, though the United States has itself signed bilateral agreements—to furnish experimental reactors—with some forty countries.

It may well be that the president, even now, could push such programs faster. He would argue that the 41 million dollars needed annually for the defense budget leaves little money for other projects. It is not entirely a question of presidential initiative. Congress each year threatens to prune the administration's foreign-aid program. Congress resisted his plan for an atom-powered merchant ship.

Mr. Eisenhower would like to see a more ambitious program for the conquest of space, but it would be a costly billion-dollar-a-year venture.

He would like to see—and has proposed—a globally coordinated drive to clear up such world-prevalent pestilences as malaria.

He would like to see laboratories delving deeper into basic research, expeditions continuing the IGY surge into the far corners of the earth.

This kind of cooperation can become irresistible, he believes. It promotes understanding between nations; it lessens tensions.

But, as of now, Mr. Eisenhower must direct his energies into other pursuits. Immediately, there has been Berlin. Allies may conduct "reconnaissance" expeditions in seeking solutions to this crisis—as Britain's Prime Minister Harold Macmillan did so helpfully at Moscow—but the big decisions are reserved for Washington to make, because of the United States' power status. In the last analysis, these decisions will be made by the president himself. As the London *Sunday Times* has commented, in writing about Mr. Eisenhower:

"The President of the United States stands at the head of the greatest single concentration of industrial and technological power in the world. By the mere fact of being elected as Chief Executive and commander in chief, an American President . . . becomes one of those upon whom the fate of all humanity may depend."

How a president mobilizes his authority, how he weaves his party strategy, how he deals in patronage and public opinion, how he utilizes even such devices as his weekly press conference—these determine whether potential power is transformed into actual leadership, and whether the office measures up to the responsibilities of a challenging age.

One cannot yet write the verdict of history on President Eisenhower. He has presided benignly over a nation at peace; he fostered a friendly climate which saw the American standard of living explosively hoisted to its highest plateau in history. He worked to detensionize the Formosa Strait.

But he was not able to remake the Republican party in his image or rejuvenate its prospects at the ballot box. He sought a *détente* at the first Geneva summit conference, but it did not come off.

Now at a time when his administration is under a constitutional sentence of expiration in less than two years and there is a new regime at the Department of State, he has to deal with the world's most formidable exponent of brinkmanship, Nikita S. Khrushchev.

For this leader of the North Atlantic Treaty Organization coalition, the task is to hold West Berlin—or through careful negotiation evolve a new status for it which does not wreck the morale and the defense posture of the Atlantic coalition.

Here, it would seem, is where history will sift most finely the qualities of judgment and initiative, as well as imperturbability and firmness, displayed by Mr. Eisenhower.

The watchword at the White House these days is "steadiness." The United States, Mr. Eisenhower has pointed out, has embarked on a long-range program of positive strength—of armament for the missile age. In the early stages of this armament program, the Soviet missile capacity will be considerably larger than the American. But in this interim period, the president firmly believes, the United States Strategic Air Command will be amply sufficient to maintain the balance of power. Its bombers are not outmoded—not yet.

The White House is confident that its armament program is sufficient to meet the Soviet threat—at least so far as American intelligence sources estimate that threat. Therefore Mr. Eisenhower believes that the American program should continue on its accustomed upward curve, and that neither Berlin nor Quemoy nor any other sudden crisis should "panic" Washington into some new crash program, or into a crisis-intensifying special mobilization of forces.

Behind this viewpoint is a feeling that any legitimate Soviet apprehensions concerning Berlin's influence on East Germany or concerning a rearmed Germany can be dissipated. But if the Soviets—if Mr. Khrushchev—is simply endeavoring by probing and more probing and by feints and brinkmanship to force the Allies out of West Berlin so that he may eventually force American power out of Europe altogether, then he will find that the United States is not budging an inch.

Is the presidential prescription for steadiness and for readiness patiently to explore ways to agreement—even at a summit conference—sufficient?

Here may develop the lasting judgment on President Eisenhower. There are other criticisms which are raised from time to time.

It is said, for example, that the president has not conferred sufficiently with that breadth of American opinion which would give him larger perspective in these churning days; that he limits his stag dinners and his close companions to successful businessmen and a few military cronies, eschewing the educators, labor representatives, and professors who might present added ideas for his consideration.

It is also suggested that he has estimated too narrowly the ability of the United States to undertake major expenditures—for defense or any other purpose—and still remain solvent. Critics complain of the influence of former Treasury Secretary George M. Humphrey and his concentrated belief that it is Communist strategy to cause the United States to spend itself into bankruptcy.

Mr. Eisenhower has had to make clear at a press conference that he does not put a balanced budget ahead of national preparedness.

In 1961—not such a distant date—President Eisenhower will be retired to private life, probably managing his acres at Gettysburg. So far, the Washington consensus is that, while historians will call him a good president and a popular one, they would also list his personal disinclination to use power strongly in time of need.

Now, peculiarly enough, the call to speak powerfully and act powerfully has come, in the final phase of the Eisenhower era.

This is not the sort of international parleying which the president would prefer. He would rather be leading a great conquest to expand mankind's knowledge or resources.

These last months and years of the Eisenhower term seem destined to see more than one major negotiating sequence with Nikita Khrushchev and the Russians. The Eisenhower-Christian Herter combination appears to be a little more flexible than the Eisenhower-Foster Dulles combination ever was. Will the new team do any better than the old team? These final months will be interesting to watch.

Can President Eisenhower in his conversations with Mr. Khrushchev—in Washington, Moscow, or elsewhere—persuade the Soviet leader to give less attention to the international expansion of communism and more attention to participation (or competition) in great global projects for the betterment of all humanity? If the president can nudge Khrushchev and his Soviet Union toward this kind of reunion with the family of man—and he would like to do so—this would undoubtedly be recorded as the greatest presidential achievement of Eisenhower the Peacemaker.

2

Khrushchev

(U.S.S.R.)

Moscow

TODAY THE West is dealing with the Soviet Union of Premier Nikita Sergeyevich Khrushchev. What is it like? Let us take a few soundings.

A group of Western diplomats and American newsmen were chewing things over in Moscow and someone asked this question:

"Suppose we display a streamlined electronic cooking range at the American Exhibition here in Skolniki Park this summer? Will the Soviets believe us when we say it's right off the assembly line, or will they insist it is something we dreamed up especially for this occasion?"

"Listen," replied an embassy official long resident in the Soviet Union, "the Russians are ready to believe anything about the American standard of living. Even that the streets are paved with gold. Of course they'll believe that this cookstove is in daily use in America."

All of which suggests one small "constant" of today's Soviet scene: the people have a continuing, avid interest in things American. In American culture, in American jazz, in the quality of American consumer goods. It is an interest displayed by Mr. Khrushchev himself. It is a reason why the Soviet people are by no means unfriendly to Americans.

One need only note the crowds which daily gathered around an ordinary Ford Fairlane sedan parked in front of my hotel, the Metropole. They apparently had never seen a streamlined auto design like that before. Or the thousands of radio listeners who tune in on "Music—U.S.A.," a Voice of America program that is never jammed and is, half of it, frankly jazz.

America is still the land at the end of the rainbow to millions of Soviet citizens.

What are some of the other "constants" of Soviet attitude and motivation?

As I am sightseeing in the vicinity of the main gate of the Kremlin, a loud bell rings. Guards come to attention; traffic is halted. A big Packard-like limousine, curtains drawn on the rear windows, speeds out of the fortressed walls and away down a side street. The curtains flutter sufficiently to disclose a solitary passenger: it could be Nikita Khrushchev.

This swift passage of the limousine is like—and yet unlike—the old Stalin days. Mr. Khrushchev is undisputed boss of the Soviet empire. Yet he does not wear Stalin's absolutist mantle; he is not deified. He deals with his Presidium colleagues on a businesslike basis, day by day—though it appears that he can always have the last persuasive word if he wishes it.

The Soviet public regards him as a man powerful enough to manage the faceless bureaucracy—to make it behave—and they want somebody at the top who is that powerful. They admire Mr. K's sharpness in foreign affairs. They applaud the way he has delivered the goods, boosted Soviet prestige with Sputnik and Lunik. They like the promises in that heady new seven-year plan.

The Soviet premier has been able to project his ebullient personality successfully. But, unlike Stalin, he cultivates Soviet public opinion, feels the need of it. He knows that there is latent opposition to some of his audacious proposals. Some folk still think he is too impetuous, too inconstant, talks too much.

So here is a second "fixed fact" of today's U.S.S.R.: the driving, dynamic Khrushchev personality, and his continuing efforts to inject his ideas, his enthusiasms, into the Soviet mind; his plans for consolidating the farm collectives, his penchant for growing corn (maize) even in a climate that produces mainly stalk and few ears; his compulsive desire to "catch up" with the United States.

At the last party congress, Mr. Khrushchev did not bother to do more than denounce the "antiparty group" as a "despicable" lot, opposed to the measures which gave the U.S.S.R. such a surge of progress. He did not bring Georgi M. Malenkov, Lazar M. Kaganovich, Vyacheslav M. Molotov, or the others to trial. He is believed to be strong enough, his position secure enough, so he can afford to be lenient.

In the present Presidium, perhaps a dozen members owe their positions directly to him. He runs the party—he has the powers of patronage. The Army has no representation at the top. The secret police is firmly subordinated.

Therefore, though some bureaucrat may be dissatisfied with the risks of the corn-growing program, or the abolition of the tractor stations, there is no way—no place—for rivalry or opposition to crystallize. Unless major disaster overtakes a major Khrushchev program, domestic or foreign, Mr. K seems safely in power. Even Peking appears to have knuckled under to his leadership.

In the ornately beautiful Soviet subway, I talk with a Soviet citizen who speaks English. "I expect you notice, these days, that many more things are for sale in the stores—more consumer goods," I say.

She hesitates a moment. "A little," she replies quietly. "There are a few more things; not many." Obviously the average Soviet citizen is not satisfied and wishes the government would hurry along those promised consumer goods. There are long queues whenever television sets—anything really colorful—go on sale.

Yet conditions are improving. Things are happening, sometimes in a heavy-handed bureaucratic way, but happening they are.

In the English-language weekly, Moscow *News,* there is a column entitled "Round the Country." Let me read you a few items:

"Alma Ata: An automatic ore-dressing plant has been built at Sokolovskoye-Sarbai in North Kazakhstan. It will be capable of handling five million tons of iron ore annually.

"Tbilisi: An underground hydropower station is to be built in the mountains of Georgia.

"Tashkent: The Uzbek Film Studios have made a documentary on the Asian-African Writers Conference held recently in Tashkent."

Other items tell of building twenty-nine diesel locomotives for the Bhilai Steel Works in India, of a new factory which is about to turn out "baby" autos (those machines driven so wildly by Italians in Rome), and so on and on.

Ride on Moscow's subway on a Sunday afternoon, and the

comfortably dressed people look not vastly different from those in Paris or London.

Almost everyone is dressed in black, and somehow I am reminded of Henry Ford's famous alleged specification that "the public can have any color Ford so long as it's black." Still, there is friendliness, purposefulness. Crowds pour into the huge skating areas at Gorki Park on Sunday morning, skating with a marvelous intensity. Small fry ride on sleds behind a troika in Skolniki Park. College students practice ski jumps on the "university heights" overlooking the Moscow River, and their serious mien suggests winners at the next Winter Olympics.

So far as I could perceive, no one looks over his shoulder, fearing the secret police. There is certainly a "thaw" in old patterns. Many cities and areas of the U.S.S.R. are decidedly more primitive than Moscow, but "change" is written all over the landscape.

In Soviet travel the visitor sees nothing, of course, of the Soviet guided-missile program—and the West should indeed be alert here. Mr. Khrushchev has come close to using "missile intimidation" in several of his major addresses. Yet other things, too, are under way inside the Soviet Union.

A few American officials were invited to a public speech by Igor Moiseyev, director of the Moiseyev dance group, which so successfully toured the United States. Mr. Moiseyev gave a glowing report on American cultural life; he praised the quality of American musicianship, he admired American restaurants, he described the range of food and services available at American stores. He said New York's atmosphere was so contagious that after a day on its streets, "I found myself running to keep up."

Several similar speeches on the United States have been made lately, and articles written: by publicist Ilya Ehrenberg (who can praise or attack at the turn of a coat) and by Stanislav Menshikov, son of the Soviet ambassador to Washington. Director Moiseyev has, however, been reprimanded for giving such praise to American institutions.

Obviously Premier Khrushchev is intrigued by the United States. Finally he has visited the United States. Note the reproachful words he used in his closing speech to the party congress: "For what crimes does the president deprive me of the right enjoyed by others to visit his country?"

Obviously he believed that an American tour, by himself, could persuade Americans that the Soviet Union is not such a dangerous opponent after all. He would pitch his personality against the United States government, seek to build up pressures to change, to disarm United States foreign policy. I believe he also had an intense curiosity simply to "see" the United States.

Was he a villain, to be deprived of an invitation on moral grounds? Washington had said as much. He "survived" in a Stalinist age when it was dog eat dog at high levels in the hierarchy. He has tried to say since then that he opposed the worst Stalinist excesses. How directly he was responsible for Ukrainian purges and the decimation of the kulaks in his areas is a matter strongly argued both ways.

The one thing to be said in Mr. Khrushchev's favor is that he moved to change the system—denounced Stalin and uprooted the power of the secret police—and he has not turned the clock back. Control by an all-powerful, all-seeing party is more benign than control by an all-powerful, all-seeing police. But Mr. K denounced only Stalin's brutality against the Communist hierarchy, not his brutality against the Russian people.

There was some speculation among foreign observers in Moscow, when First Deputy Premier Anastas I. Mikoyan was dining with bankers in New York, that the Soviet supersalesman was actually seeking to discover the whereabouts of the "real government" of the United States—that alleged inner "Presidium" or politburo which really runs the United States, presumably from Wall Street. Others scoffed at the idea that the shrewd Armenian could be so taken in by communism's own folklore.

But the story does emphasize how the Soviet Union itself is indeed ruled by an inner circle, the Presidium, and the party elite. The Communist party is acutely aware of the importance of power, of choosing the right men to stand for the one-slate election in every district, every republic, acutely aware of the need to maintain singleness of purpose, a monolithic opinion, an effective chain of command.

In a land where no opposition party—or even opinion—is allowed to flourish, can one hope for liberalization, for less rigidity?

Talk with some of the American students now studying in the U.S.S.R., and they will tell you that Soviet students are not—now—sources of discontent. There is occasionally a little griping but there are no firebrands. Those who are troublemakers can so easily be deprived of scholarships and tuition. Economic persuasion is very effective.

Meanwhile, the members of the intelligentsia, the engineers, natural scientists, teachers, factory managers—from four to eight million of them—have been largely neutralized politically. They receive more awards, better housing; some can

Eisenhower *Converse*

Wide World Photos **Khrushchev**

Macmillan *Converse*

U.P.I. Photo **De Gaulle**

Adenauer *Converse*

Wide World Photos **Gomulka** **Tito** *Wide World Photos*

Bourguiba *Converse*

Converse **Nasser**

Nkrumah *Converse*

Ben-Gurion *Converse*

U Nu *Converse*

Converse **Sukarno**

Garcia *Wide World Photos*

Converse **Rahman**

Kishi

Converse

Converse

Chiang

travel abroad. But they are generally engrossed in their work, they simply are not politically minded, and they want to hold their positions.

The very unwillingness of Mr. Khrushchev and the party to allow Soviet artists to establish independent criteria or criticism shows the system at work. The party believes it cannot permit even a small independence of critical judgment, lest the society be atomized. Hence the abuse meted out to the novelist Boris Pasternak.

"Still, there is some danger—long-range—to the system in merely having educated people around," declares an astute American observer. "As these educated people enter the higher levels of the hierarchy, their less rigid ideas may begin to take hold. Khrushchev is from a generation brought up during the revolution. As such he is more free thinking than Stalin was, but he is inhibited by his past and his upbringing.

"The next generation may be more liberal. Anything can happen in the Soviet Union if it happens at the top first. Witness the startling campaign which demoted Stalin. But if the top ranks of the party see what they consider to be an unhealthy development anywhere, they will mobilize all the party's resources to squelch it."

What about Soviet foreign policy? It is never very clear what the minimum Soviet terms are. But if we were to ask Mr. Khrushchev what the Soviet role in world affairs is today, we might hazard that he would reply in this wise:

"The role of the Soviet Union is to prove that the Communist system is dynamically effective in building a powerful modern state, in satisfying the basic urges of a great people. We are succeeding marvelously; capitalism is doomed."

This Soviet system will be something to contend with, as

time marches on. Asked what is most encouraging within the U.S.S.R., Mr. Khrushchev might well refer to the success of his ambitious programs to decentralize industry, to plow up the steppes, to produce a new, more businesslike, more incentive-conscious farming system. His dynamic ideas are doing well on these fronts.

He perhaps would not wish to recognize that, in the degree that he frees the Soviet system and gives more scope to individual initiative, his system will succeed even better than it has in the past. He may not recognize that, despite the campaigns against "revisionism," the next generation of Soviet leaders will be even more revisionist than he has been—and he has been quite revisionist himself.

3

Macmillan

(GREAT BRITAIN)

London

PRIME MINISTER Harold Macmillan has a dash of the the bold Elizabethan Age about him.

He has more than once compared today's resourceful Britain, under Elizabeth II, to the small daring nation of Elizabeth I.

His outlook favors the same boldness, the same imperturbability, the same expansiveness, the same high confidence of those earlier days.

In an age when Britain is again physically small, between two nuclear giants, history can be reassuring.

Meet Mr. Macmillan at No. 10 Downing Street, or in his offices in Parliament's inner sanctum, and you discover an unruffled sense which is not always associated with politicians, even astute ones. It bespeaks a very strong belief that Britain will be on hand, playing its civilizing role in world affairs, far down the future.

What is this civilizing role?

Let us ask Mr. Macmillan as he sits at ease at the great table in the prime minister's office within the House of Commons, a table large enough for a Cabinet meeting. Here is that Edwardian mustache trimmed down to size, here is that slightly dandified air, that touch of whimsicality—behind which nevertheless looms an impression of confidence, of power, of experience, of accumulated wisdom.

One can understand how, when Mr. Macmillan began to "come through" to the British people—on the platform, over the television—his popularity graph moved readily upward.

What is Britain's civilizing destiny? Mr. Macmillan puts it this way:

"We have a unique fund of practical experience—accumulated through many years—in developing human institutions to conform with human ideals. For instance, no country has played a greater part in the evolution of parliamentary government, or the growth of the common law, or the development of those judicial safeguards of the individual.

"These institutions have stood the test of time and changing circumstances. They have been adopted by other countries, including the great countries of the Commonwealth which we have helped to nationhood."

The prime minister might simply have said: Look at the map of the world!

And if we did so, we would see parliamentary government flourishing in India, the common law adopted in the courts of Pakistan, a British-trained civil service in Malaya, and a whole proud array of governmental and judicial institutions "made in Britain" being introduced today in the new Commonwealth countries of Ghana, the West Indies Federation, and Nigeria.

This contribution of what may be termed "democratic institutions"—tailored differently in different countries to suit varying conditions and degrees of maturity—is quite a gift to mankind, quite a good-will offering from one small island kingdom whose numbers have never stretched beyond the 50 million mark.

Mr. Macmillan was in a relaxed mood; it had been a busy day in Parliament. Now, in early evening, he was awaiting a Commons vote—a "division"—on a minor matter. Musing out loud, he sought to delve down to the value of these British contributions.

"The object of it all, I suppose," he said, "is to make a better individual human life. The old values still ring true, would you not agree? Man's duty to God and to his neighbor . . . what man owes to the society in which he lives.

"Do we have faith in our own way of life? I believe that in two or three generations even the people of the Soviet Union will be asking themselves these same fundamental questions.

"They will ask: 'What is human life for? Who put us here?' Questions of that sort—spiritual, searching.

"The Russians are allowing the human mind to be applied to science and knowledge and skills—on the one side—while attempting to exclude from it anything savoring of free inquiry and discussion. I believe that if you open up the mind to one subject, you cannot keep it closed to other subjects forever."

There is another side to British achievement that the prime minister is also ready to stress, and this, too, has an Elizabethan flavor. It is the material accomplishments of prosperous Britain today.

"If you ask what is the most hopeful internal development in Britain today, I would say that it is the fact we have been able to keep to the very forefront of industrial achievement and inventiveness," he said. "To give a few examples, we are playing a leading role in the development of the uses of nuclear energy for peaceful purposes. We are forging ahead in the aircraft, electric, electronic, and chemical industries.

"It is not too much to say that we are experiencing a second Industrial Revolution ourselves, and its effects throughout the world may well equal those of the first."

There is not the slightest doubt that Britain is again proving that it can "deliver the goods" in the way of nuclear power plants, huge turbines, radar gear, petro-chemical industries, advanced machine tools and technology—the really advanced industry and engineering of this half of the twentieth century.

Favoring financial winds from the Macmillan government, including a reduction in Britain's burdensome income tax, have helped this resurgence to continue. The prime minister believes in Britain and he believes in the future. He is an expansionist and a natural optimist. When others were bewailing what the fortunes of Suez had done to Britain, Mr. Macmillan, as the new prime minister, began talking about the authentic greatness of Britain. And he set about reviving that greatness.

The prime minister believes that Britain's material future lies in a developing Commonwealth, a vanguard position in industrial progress, an alert investment program at home and abroad, lowered taxation, and a boost in consumer spending power.

To a degree this has worked, and prosperity is brightly evident in Britain today, a striking comparison with even two and three years ago. But unemployment has been rising here and there, and inflation once again threatens. No Western government has really solved the problem of how to free investment capital and consumer spending, and yet avoid inflation.

What is certain is that Mr. Macmillan, by personal qualities and personal drive, has put the Conservative party's prospects way ahead of what people expected when he came to office on the resignation of Sir Anthony Eden as prime minister. Billed first as a mere "stopgap" prime minister, he, like his country, has delivered the goods.

He said Britain's recovery would continue, and it did. He said the Anglo-American alliance should be revived, and he proceeded to develop a close personal relationship with President Eisenhower; Anglo-American relations are at their best in many years. He decided that nuclear sharing by the United States should move ahead faster; it has.

It is like the days of 1951 when, on the accession of the Conservatives to power, Minister of Housing Macmillan was given the task of building 300,000 homes in a year. Labor said it could not be done. Unorthodox Mr. Macmillan did it.

The prime minister is a product of Eton, Balliol College at Oxford, and the Guards Brigade. In some of his earlier years, he devoted himself largely to the Macmillan publishing fortunes. From 1925 to 1940 he sat in the House of Commons, with only a short break, with no offers of government posts or preferment from the Tories of those days. While Tory governments were uncomprehending, he tried to do something about the dire unemployment between the wars; in 1936 he warned of the rise of Hitler. His party did not heed.

It was Sir Winston Churchill, another Tory rebel, who brought him into the government—making him minister resident at Allied headquarters in North Africa, where he came to know General Dwight D. Eisenhower intimately. Here among intricate diplo-military problems he grew as a statesman.

He has since served as foreign minister and chancellor of the exchequer. His common sense, his housing accomplishments, his optimism recommended him. When Sir Anthony resigned, it seemed the natural thing to call on unruffled Mr. Macmillan.

In early 1959 he went on a "reconnaissance" to Moscow, not quite with the blessing of Washington, but certainly without its frown. He had no intention thereby of weakening the Anglo-American alliance; he holds that never again must the two countries be divided. But he believes persistently that an exploration of Soviet purposes will do no harm, nor will a flexibility of position whenever the West goes to a conference table with Moscow.

Mr. Macmillan's domestic success, after his wilderness years, is a British political phenomenon. Surely it is due in part to the fact that he has matched the British mood of these years: purposeful, bold, ready for new paths.

This is the Britain which has poured heavy investment into foreign-aid programs. "In recent years our record has been second only to that of your own country," he reminded me. This is the Britain which works creatively for peace. "The Anglo-American alliance is designed to serve the world, not to establish a hegemony," he comments.

And this is the Britain which, in a new Elizabethan Age, is again proving that its contributions to mankind—the outpourings from Westminster, Oxford, Harwell, Birmingham, Cambridge, Edinburgh, Jodrell Bank (the names ring out like the chimes of Big Ben!)—are as rich and varied as those of any past century.

4

De Gaulle

(FRANCE)

Paris

THE FIRST time I saw General Charles de Gaulle he was holding a press conference in a drafty Paris *salon* late in 1944. Clad in a military greatcoat—for no Paris building was well warmed in those chill post-liberation days—he was enunciating government policy. He undoubtedly believed then that his hour of greatness had struck. But his ministers refused to follow him. He was destined to wait another fourteen years.

Earlier in 1944, he had participated in a Paris memorial service. Suddenly shots were fired by a stray Nazi or a Communist renegade. People rushed to take cover. But not General de Gaulle. Believing in his mission, unruffled, untouched, he marched ahead, eyes high.

He has displayed this same sense of mission, this mystique, this imperturbability ever since.

Much has happened just as he forecast. On New Year's Eve, 1944, shortly before he quit the new-formed government, he issued a severe warning to the parliamentary leaders who were beginning to behave "like the Third Republic" all over again:

"If you do not take into account the absolute necessities for governmental authority, dignity, and responsibility, you will proceed to such a situation that one day or another, I predict to you, you will bitterly regret having taken the course you will have taken."

The crisis finally arrived—with the Algerian war costing France 2 million dollars a day, with the Army in virtual revolt, the Assembly frustrated, the finances scrambled. And General de Gaulle was recalled to power—he who wrote in his memoirs:

"I was convinced that France would have to go through gigantic trials; that the interest of life consisted in one day rendering her some signal service, and that I would have the occasion to do so."

It is really remarkable that this leader was there, ready. Surely it would have been difficult to find a substitute. And because he was at hand, talk of civil war, anxieties, fighting at the barricades—all evaporated. Not everyone in France has embraced General de Gaulle with enthusiasm. There is still a surprising amount of apathy and self-concern among the French people. But with him in power, France has its new opportunity for greatness.

What is there about Charles de Gaulle? How could he march calmly amid bullets, epithets, dashed hopes, suspicions? One must quote again, from his memoirs, that passage which now is becoming familiar, where he says that his emotional side tends to imagine France "like the princess in the fairy stories" as dedicated to "an exalted and exceptional destiny."

"Instinctively I have the feeling that providence has created her either for complete successes or for exemplary misfortunes. . . . But the positive side of my mind also assures me that France is not really herself unless in the front rank; that only vast enterprises are capable of counterbalancing the ferments of dispersal which are inherent in her people; that our country . . . must aim high and hold itself straight, on pain of mortal danger.

"In short, to my mind, France cannot be France without greatness."

Nothing could be more indicative of President de Gaulle's character and outlook than these words. They are a constant guide to his conduct. They suggest that he believes he is an instrument of history, an instrument of unselfed service to his ideal. And this at a time in world history when the general Western tendency is toward mediocrity of utterance and a downplaying of sentiment! He is a refreshing phenomenon on the world stage.

But there could—there still can—be danger and difficulty in an inflated attitude of *"la gloire,"* of French grandeur and place in the sun, although something of this sentiment has been vastly needed after the humiliations of the war years.

The most hopeful aspect of the Gaullist phenomenon is the way this man has developed policy since taking office—the way he has penetrated the Laocoön tangle of French problems.

Premier (and later President) de Gaulle dealt first with the Army, restoring the sovereignty of civil authority, gradually shifting the Algerian hotheads to other commands, gradually calming the situation. The Army may not forget that it effectively intervened politically in French affairs, but for now it is "disarmed."

Again, remembering the dubious authority of his Free French movement in World War II, General de Gaulle quickly obtained and wrapped a cloak of legality around his assumption of power. He has caused to be written—a decade and a half late!—the kind of constitution that he feels is necessary for France, giving major power to the executive branch, and reducing the Assembly's mischief-making proclivities.

Again, though no financial wizard himself, he has managed to rebuild basically France's self-defeating financial structure. He has produced a harder franc, raised taxes, cut down the heavy subsidies and pensions—made it less possible for France to self-deceive itself about its finances. He is moving to lift some of the protection from protectionist-minded industry.

As for Algeria, the greatest challenge of all, President de Gaulle has made a powerful effort to place the rebels on the psychological defensive, offering amnesties, proposing a common association of France and Algeria, raising everyone's sights by a five-year economic development which includes Sahara oil.

Like a Delphic oracle, he has said something hopeful—but not too plainly—to each faction: rebels, colons, metropolitan Frenchmen, Army. He wants five years in which to attempt to weave a delicate compromise. Whether he can do it, whether time will hold still, is another question.

What we do see here is a France which has the opportunity to recover faith in itself, through a leader who has faith in France.

I would have liked to have asked President de Gaulle to spell out his views of France's individual role in world affairs. But at present he sees no newspaper correspondents. Perhaps he has said and written so much on the topic already that a further question and answer would be superfluous.

Surely France's role, as President de Gaulle sees it, is to be one of the great nations of the world, and perhaps the leading nation of Europe. Its role is to work in harmony with its allies. Its role is to develop a "commonwealth," "community," or close association with its colonies. Its role is never to surrender its nationhood to any supranational "European federation." France's destiny is nationalistic, in the eyes of President de Gaulle.

Is there indeed some peril of international misunderstanding here? Surely, close observers feel, the danger is that France might aim for an ascendancy beyond its abilities and power to maintain—and in the end become embittered because friends and allies failed to give quite the same heed to French "glory" that its partisans believe is due.

This need not happen. President de Gaulle is a realist. He is expected to hold in check the more extreme demands of some of his devoted followers, including able, attractive Premier Michel Debré, whose appointment indicates that "le grand Charles" intends to exercise close supervision of every aspect of national policy.

M. Debré, a resistance fighter, and recently the minister of justice who largely framed the new constitution, has in the past been stridently nationalist. He has expressed sharp opposition to "European" concepts which involved any surrender of sovereignty, such as the European Defense Community, against which he fought successfully. He has opposed any French "pull-out" from any overseas territories, protectorates, or spheres of influence.

Yet, since he assumed office under President de Gaulle—since he has been in power instead of in opposition and since he has been directly under tutelage—he has modified some of his extreme statements. He does not oppose "European" solutions, such as the Common Market—so long as the national participants remain nations and do not merge themselves into some kind of European federation. Collaboration must always be by sovereign states, he holds.

Still, President de Gaulle, Premier Debré, and the fervent members of their new party, the Union for a New Republic, must decide how far they can go in demanding more prestige for France. Nationalism, retained sovereignty, may be the present solution for France. But how much "grandeur," extra prestige, must go with it?

Militarily, France aspires under President de Gaulle to a larger role in the North Atlantic Treaty Organization. France would be spokesman for the Western European continent in NATO. France wants NATO strategy to embrace overseas areas, including North Africa.

Premier Debré says France has "the duty of becoming an atomic military power," that this is a "necessity for France and for Europe." And that France has "the duty of calling attention to the unparalleled, strategic importance of the French position in the Mediterranean."

What does this mean? Is atomic power to be the talisman by which France lays claim to special greatness? If so, how will reviving Western Germany—whose leader, Konrad Adenauer, has made many concessions to France in the interests of common harmony—how will Germany react to future French claims for pre-eminence? There are observers who see seeds of future discord right here.

Meanwhile, encouragingly, President de Gaulle has indeed embraced those two main designs for European economic collaboration: the Common Market, and the Coal-Steel Community. He has said that France "must emerge from her closed economy and participate." On the Euratom (atomic-energy pooling) he has been noncommittal.

The great difference between de Gaulle and Debré, on the one hand, and European federalists like Paul-Henri Spaak, on the other, is that the federalists see these economic mergers as the first step toward political merger. President de Gaulle, on the other hand, wants no "European" parliament, no "European" executive authority.

Time and experience may mellow the French viewpoint. But France has never regarded federation as enthusiastically as some of its neighbors, and it is unlikely to change its sentiments under President de Gaulle.

Europe—and the Atlantic Alliance and the Common Market—all need a strong France. If only the Algerian drain can be ended, France's energies can be bent creatively and more lavishly in more constructive directions. The hope in the French position today lies in the devotion, the enthusiasm, and the expertise which General de Gaulle has brought into the picture.

Fifteen years ago—as the forlorn tank expert who had retreated courageously to Britain to carry on the struggle when Marshal Pétain surrendered—he was much more unyielding, much less deft, less aware of the currents and swirls of French politics.

But in the busy years since the war he has been a kind of father image—retired in his village—to which Gaullists, socialists, former presidents, ambassadors, generals, all sorts of people, came for talk and counsel. He became consequently perhaps the best-informed man in France. Writing his memoirs, thinking over his first try at French government, he saw mistakes, revised estimates, charted different courses.

The son of a schoolteacher at a Jesuit school, a graduate of St. Cyr military academy, former advocate of Panzer blitzkrieg to a France engrossed with its Maginot Line complex, de Gaulle now has become a consummate politician.

It will be interesting to watch his search for Algerian solutions, his well-begun efforts to strengthen French finances, his role in the strategy to defend Berlin, his future behavior toward the Common Market.

There are still absurd suspicions among some of his followers that the United States, somehow, is scheming to take North Africa away from France, including the Sahara oil—even as General de Gaulle once suspected Winston Churchill of seeking to acquire portions of the French colonial empire. But President de Gaulle is likely to restrain his hotheads in such matters.

General de Gaulle once wrote: "So true it is that, face to face with the great perils, the only salvation lies in greatness." How will this tall, austere, perceptive leader utilize his concept of French "greatness"? It is possible for a European nation, freed of colonies and colonial drains, to emerge more prosperous than before, as Britain has shown. Greatness can be a fetish if it leads to quixotic adventures.

But the careful, thoughtful course which President de Gaulle has set so far leads to confidence that his compass is not overly fixed on a false star. If French self-interest and his opponents do not bring him down by mean and petty strategies, there is hope that President de Gaulle can lead France to a greatness that will not be Napoleonic, but in the finer traditions of European, Atlantic, and "commonwealth" brotherhood.

5

Adenauer

(WEST GERMANY)

Bonn

WAGGING A serious forefinger, much as a schoolmaster might do in instructing a pupil, Chancellor Konrad Adenauer quickly staked out the destiny of his nation as he saw it. "Germany's mission in this epoch," he said, as we sat in his chastely beautiful office in Bonn's Schaumburg Palace beside the Rhine, "is to help safeguard and preserve the Christian character of Western Europe."

A large order? Yet no knowledgeable person here doubts that this objective, in its widest meaning, is the role in which this remarkably durable, single-purposed leader of the Federal German Republic has sought to cast his country.

This is why, according to his own judgment, the West must stand resolutely firm against the shrewd Soviet proposals on Berlin and German unification. In each case, Chancellor Adenauer argues, the ultimate deadly aim is to penetrate and "communize" Germany—therefore to render it impotent in the role he has envisioned for it.

In medieval times the Germanic peoples helped thwart aggression from the East. Dr. Adenauer approves the view of

Gibbon, the historian, that Germany's role is to hold the line against barbarism. Of course, Germany itself has resorted to barbaric war in recent times. But no one, surveying the policies of this chancellor who has held office longer than any democratic leader of Europe, has the slightest doubt that the Germany he wants to perpetuate is one linked to the West economically, allied to the West militarily, and breaking bread with the West culturally.

"These ties are requisite," Dr. Adenauer commented, now wagging a didactic pencil, now implacably solemn, now displaying a delicate humor with twinkling eyes.

"If Germany were in, say, the geographical position of Spain, we might not require these ties. But Germany is in the middle, between a hostile scheming East, and the Allied West."

There are those who believe that Dr. Adenauer is more interested in a strong Federal Republic integrated with the West than he is in a reunification of his domain with Prussia. Actually, German reunification is not the flaming issue in the prosperous Federal Republic that the Soviets or the Americans appear to believe.

I had listed, as possible ties to the West, the Common Market, the Coal-Steel Community, and Euratom. "Add NATO to the list," he quickly replied without waiting for the translator to repeat my question in German, thus revealing both an active concern for the Western military alliance and a fair knowledge of English.

One might ask precisely what Chancellor Adenauer means by maintaining the "Christian character" of Europe. He is a Roman Catholic; he maintains a careful balance between Protestant and Roman Catholic in his own Christian Democratic party.

The chancellor's next answer made clear that he was thinking in wide nondenominational terms. He had been asked what incident, what domestic development in this thriving German nation was most encouraging to him.

"After the war," he answered, "Germany had to buckle down and work extremely hard to build the material goods necessary for life and survival. I was afraid that by their impressive achievements the German people might be deviated from a concern for the nonmaterial aspects of life.

"But in the last one or two years there has been a very clear development of the nonmaterial side. And this is the case with our young people particularly. By nonmaterial I mean spiritual values, artistic and cultural values, religious values, respect for history.

"Prosperity does not always promote a seeking after spiritual values," he said, again gesturing with his pencil, "nor does poverty. A right balance is needed between prosperity and other concerns."

To anyone arriving in Western Germany from the Communist East, the prosperity everywhere evident is striking. Bonn, in its quiet setting beside the swift-flowing broad Rhine, seems more a provincial capital, despite the new government buildings, than it does the governing city of a vibrant, dramatically recovered nation. But one need only travel to the near-by Ruhr to discover, amid the smoking chimneys and roar of machinery, why West Germany has risen in ten short years to become the most powerful industrial country in continental Western Europe.

But now, despite the recovery record and the vast popularity this has given to Chancellor Adenauer who has presided over the swift ascent, the Adenauer policy of "holding firm" against efforts to discover new solutions for German unification, and new formulas for beleaguered Berlin's status, has come into question.

Moscow has revived its proposal for a confederation of the Federal Republic and its shabby Eastern "People's Republic," 50 million Western Germans setting up loose central ties with 17 million Germans of the Soviet zone. What did Dr. Adenauer think of the Soviet proposal? He had a short pithy answer:

"Can you confederate fire and water?"

He continued, "Just read what East Germany's Ulbricht says—see how he envisions confederation. He has said he wants a 'free hand' in the Federal Republic.

"The Russian proposal for a German peace treaty—creating a demilitarized, neutralized Germany—has the same aim. They would turn the Federal Republic gradually into a Communist state.

"Grotewohl said at Peking that soon the red flag would fly over the whole of Germany."

"What of Berlin?" I asked the chancellor. Moscow has proposed that the West's rail and road communications with the beleaguered city be transferred from Soviet to East German hands, with possibly some kind of United Nations "guarantee" of the independent status of the city.

How did the chancellor see the Berlin issue? Would it be a good idea to station West German troops in Berlin, as some have proposed?

"Stationing our troops in Berlin would only complicate the situation—make matters worse. Berlin actually is being defended outside of Berlin by the common policy and the determination of the Allied powers."

Then the chancellor—leaning forward—launched into an explanation of his basic view on unification.

"There has not been sufficient understanding of the Soviet initiative," he said. "The partition of Germany is not the cause of world tension but the consequence of tension. Partition resulted from the tensions developed years ago among the four powers governing Germany—the fact that two opponents faced each other, the United States and the U.S.S.R. Reunification of Germany would not eliminate this tension.

"This tension can only be eliminated by a system of controlled disarmament, in both the nuclear and conventional fields."

I asked the chancellor his views on the Rapacki Plan, launched by Poland with Moscow's backing, proposing a denuclearized, neutralized zone across the center of Europe and embracing Poland, Czechoslovakia, and both Germanys.

"A disarmed Germany," he sternly answered, "would be a disaster for the West. In the long run, it would only increase dangerously the economic power of the Soviet Union.

"The Soviets have not abandoned their aim to capture Western Europe, and of course all of Germany. They intend to become the world's most powerful economic power.

"Not many months ago the Common Market published a survey on the economic potential of various countries for 1957. If you set the economic potential of the United States at twenty, then that of the six nations of the Common Market totals seventeen. Now suppose Moscow, by its peace proposals, succeeds in expanding communism in the Federal Republic. This would destroy European integration. Eventually the Soviets would get a hold on the economic potential of the

180 million people in the six countries. . . . This would have the gravest political and economic consequences.

"It is completely wrong not to take into account the long-range objectives of the Russians. Experts say the West frequently underestimates the distant goals of the Soviets."

The immensely complex question to be resolved by the West today is whether Moscow actually wants a German settlement—or a European settlement—dearly enough to be willing to make realistic concessions to obtain it. Is Dr. Adenauer, who holds German foreign policy so completely in the palm of his hand, prepared to risk any concessions in turn—concessions which might at least form the basis for lengthy and careful four-power negotiations?

"I have nothing against a four-power conference," he commented, "but I reiterate that the German unification issue is not basically what divides the world.

"It is most strange that at this moment, when negotiations have been proceeding at Geneva on nuclear testing, and when the Anglo-Saxon powers would like to make concessions, the Soviet Union is creating new tensions at Berlin."

"But do you see any signs of a Soviet 'thaw' in any quarter, as Soviet Premier Nikita S. Khrushchev is frequently hinting?" I asked the German chancellor.

"Developments are possible in the Soviet Union, yes. It is possible that the Russians will suddenly realize that their conquest schemes are not worth while—even in the realm of economic conquest.

"However," Dr. Adenauer continued, "Mr. Khrushchev now is seeking to turn the clock back on his scientists and engineers—the rising new classes—by ordaining that their children must work in factories as the price of their education. The elite are being returned to the worker class in a generation."

The chancellor had obviously done an immense amount of thinking on the problem of Soviet relations. His opinions had largely emerged ramrod-straight, unbending. The Soviet leaders do not relish him—but cannot topple him.

He is Germany's strong man—believing firmly in democracy but conditioned by his long tenure as burgomaster of Cologne to practice one-man leadership. He has no use for the haggling brand of parliamentarianism which wrecked the prewar Weimar Republic.

During the Hitler years he was frequently persecuted, though he took no part in conspiratorial activities. In 1944 the Allies reinstated him as Cologne burgomaster, and then the British dismissed him. Whereupon he founded the Christian Democratic party and in 1949 began his amazing career as West Germany's chancellor. His first election was a narrow squeak, but, when West Germany, under his leadership, began the trek to full independence and bounding recovery, his election victories became massive.

Where now is West Germany headed? Can a dynamic nation be rendered neutral and impotent militarily? Or can Dr. Adenauer's will hold steady and West Germany slowly increase the caliber of those armaments which make the history-minded Soviets so uneasy? Or will some more modest compromise be discovered at some eventual East-West conference?

As of this writing, it does not appear that Dr. Adenauer will voluntarily open the door to compromise. His hand may be forced. Conceivably, he may be circumvented. But when the historians search their annals to discover who it was in the postwar decades that led Germany into "good" paths and sought steadily, patiently, and with civilized demeanor to anchor it finally into the West's great family, that accolade must go to Konrad Adenauer.

6

Gomulka

(POLAND)

Warsaw

THERE IS a long-argued difference of opinion among Western observers and diplomats in this bravely rebuilt Polish capital today. It is a debate about where Poland is trending. Is Poland "holding its own" against Moscow's demands and the strait-jacketing habits of its own Communist leadership? Or is Poland being slowly reeled back into Communist conformity and indistinguishability from the other Soviet satellites?

Which is it?

Is this country going to be able to maintain at least a minimum of those freedoms which opened up grandly before it in the heady days of the bloodless "October revolution" of 1956? Or will these freedoms be gradually eroded as Party Secretary Wladyslaw Gomulka falls more and more into lock step with Soviet Premier Nikita S. Khrushchev?

The American diplomats and newsmen in Warsaw, by and large, tend to believe that the road is not curving back toward Moscow—that farmers, writers, churchmen, the men-in-the-street will continue to enjoy their present liberties. Others in the diplomatic and news corps think it is just impossible for communism to permit the present state of affairs—that is, unless Mr. Khrushchev himself goes "revisionist" anew and loosens the satellite reins all around, which seems at present unlikely.

This is an important argument—if only because Poland's role in world affairs in these troublous years seems to be that of an "Exhibit A" designed to show whether or not a satellite country can free itself, to a degree, and without bloodshed, from the Communist yoke as fashioned by Moscow—and get away with it.

It would be useful if Mr. Gomulka—who was a hero to the Polish people when he assumed power after the stirring surges of October, 1956—would frankly tell us how he thinks Poland is trending, and what his own hopes and objectives may be.

But Mr. Gomulka steadily refuses to see any foreign newsmen these days, and indeed seldom sees individually any Polish reporters.

This is too bad, because Mr. Gomulka is a modest man (living in an unpretentious apartment) who is undoubtedly trying to do his best, according to his lights, to carry a so recently impoverished Poland along the recovery road—yet making sure that the party runs things.

He reputedly has a trace of anti-intellectualism in his makeup and, as is the case with most Eastern European leaders, a large amount of insularity, displayed in his unawareness of the advantages of an interview with a Western journalist.

Anyway I did not get to see the first secretary of the ruling Polish United Workers (Communist) party. Thus I could not ask him to spell out Poland's role in foreign affairs, or to throw light on the argument regarding Poland's future course. However, I have talked with Polish officials, discussed matters with Polish journalists, asked the opinion of Western diplomats and newsmen here. From these soundings, let us see what emerges.

To begin with, there are many signs in this capital city that Poland, with or without the approval of Mr. Gomulka and his presidium, has cut a large hole in the curtain which seals off the Communist bloc from Western ideas.

Western books and periodicals, including even *Vogue* magazine, are on sale at bookstores on Nowy Swiat, the main thoroughfare. There was even a recent proposal—now abandoned—to publish *Dr. Zhivago* here.

The *Times,* of London, and the Paris edition of the New York *Herald Tribune* rest on the reading table of the Bristol Hotel, along with publications from Eastern Europe.

A few dozen privately owned shops, offering such amenities as electric flatirons, Western cosmetics, chic women's hats, permanent waves, and men's tailoring, have sprung up almost within the shadow of the Palace of Culture—a skyscraper of heavy Russo-Victorian architecture which was the unsolicited postwar gift of the Soviet Union.

Twelve hundred miles eastward in Moscow, at a recent ambitious exhibit of the painting and sculpture of the "people's democracies," the Polish section was easily the liveliest, freshest, most visited, most controversial—replete with impressionist and abstract paintings—a startling invasion of "Old Ma Pravda's" domain.

These indicia do suggest that Poland has broken loose from the Communist rigidities. And most certainly everyone agrees that Poland is the freest of the Soviet satellites. But how free?

One must not conclude too much.

Some optimists and many Poles—after the headlong rout of the "Stalinists" and the inconclusive flight to Warsaw by Mr. Khrushchev, that glorious October of 1956—expected that Poland would become a kind of halfway house between Soviet communism and Western democracy.

These hopes have been dashed.

It would be more accurate to call Poland a "quarter-way house" out of the Soviet bloc. To many Poles this is bitterly disappointing.

At the same time, this correspondent, taking note of the available evidence, believes that the American thesis is the correct one: that Poland today is not being bent, nor is it drifting, into a further recessive curtailment of its minimum liberties.

The discouragement easily discoverable in Poland today stems from the great expectations which the October revolution raised. But it is quite evident that neither Mr. Gomulka nor his henchmen intended to let the revolution get too far out of hand.

It is even probable that Mr. Gomulka assured Soviet Premier Khrushchev, when he made that hasty flight to Warsaw in October, that while Poland might move more slowly toward the desired Communist goals, yet it would not abandon those goals. And that in foreign policy Poland would chart no separate course as Yugoslavia had done.

But when one looks to see whether Poland is reverting to the "bad old days," there are three main indicators to be examined:

1. Have the secret police resumed their activity?

2. Has the government begun persecution of the Roman Catholic Church?

3. Has the effort to force the farmers into collectives been renewed—an effort abandoned in 1956?

All the answers here are negative.

"Any knock at the door at 3 A.M. is still the milkman," a Polish journalist will smilingly assure you. "I can talk with you, an American newspaperman, and I will not be visited by the police today, or at any time later."

Says another Polish journalist: "I regularly attend functions at Western embassies; I fraternize with Western newsmen and officials. Show me a Soviet reporter in Moscow who does the same."

It is a known fact that Communist party Secretary Gomulka has a vast dislike for the ways of the secret police. He prefers to persuade by argument, not to enforce by terror. In conversation he seldom says, "You are to do this." Rather does he smooth the way by remarking, "Now in my view, this would be the way to do it."

Poland has in Mr. Gomulka a man of integrity, and no tyrant, though no longer a hero to the people.

What about church-state relations?

An uneasy stabilization exists today between the Polish government and the Roman Catholic Church, to which most Poles belong. But it is a stabilization, something more than an uneasy "truce," because it is based on agreement reached between the two in 1956. In effect the government has said to the church: "Obey this agreement to the letter, and we will not persecute."

Sniping from both sides continues sporadically.

But there is no war on religion in Poland.

What about the farmers? The Gomulka government has made no effort to reintroduce compulsion or strong persuasion against the peasantry to join collectives. The Polish farmer is a free man, and only 10 per cent of the farmers are in collectives.

Mr. Gomulka apparently believes that Poland will embrace socialism eventually without compulsion. He is not in favor of forcing the farmers; most certainly he would have nothing to do with a system of communes or a Stalinized treatment of the peasants.

But Poland has paid a price for its limited degree of freedom. That price is in the realm of free expression. Much more than a year ago the government closed down, amidst rioting, the student newspaper in Warsaw, *Pro Postu*. Today it carefully controls the Polish press. Some of the journals which sprang up in the heyday of "new freedom" have had to shut up shop. A few proscribed journalists find it difficult to get any of their writing accepted. In a country where many people have to work at two jobs to make ends meet, this creates serious hardship.

What is restricted, censored? Any criticism of Soviet policy. Any sharp disagreement with the government. A man may say to friends in conversation, quietly or loudly, what he cannot say in print.

The creative arts, too, are affected, in that art forms must also avoid criticism of big brother Ivan. But as the Polish exhibit at Moscow showed, Polish art flourishes despite the handicap.

Some roads to Western-style freedoms are absolutely closed in Poland. Private enterprise is unlikely to progress further than the relatively few small shops clustered near the Palace of Culture. Taxation is too high, government policy is too unfriendly, goods to sell are too hard to obtain in a state-run economy.

Mr. Gomulka is against free enterprise. Perhaps he doesn't understand how far it has evolved in Europe and America. Certainly he is known to feel that Poland "cannot afford it." To ardent Marxists it is unthinkable that such a vital and basic means of production as a steel or cement plant should be in the hands of private individuals instead of the state.

The Marxist zealots in the Gomulka regime will continue to try to force a Communist march. A recently proposed amendment to the Communist party statute says that only "purposeful criticism" may now be voiced in Poland. This sort of thing, if enacted, plus the curbs on press freedom, could indeed spell further retrogression.

Those who believe that the trend is still not backward are relying on the natural ebullience of the Polish people, their Western heritage, and their love of freedom to keep the mental atmosphere relatively free. Despite the news curbs, people will talk. Despite the resignation to "following Gomulka's road" in Polish-Soviet relations, Western and American books and ideas will be read and sought.

In foreign policy, it is well realized here that the presence of two and a half Soviet divisions on Polish soil, ostensibly to guard the line of march into East Germany, means that Poland must toe the Moscow global line. To attempt to behave like Hungary would be to suffer the fate of Hungary. So Mr. Gomulka travels about the Soviet Union in brotherly comradeship with Mr. Khrushchev, denounces "American imperialism," and reluctantly approves the execution of Hungary's Imre Nagy.

Polish journalists claim this is expediency. Poland dare not disagree with Moscow. They also recall that Poland would like to keep those war-won ex-German territories and that only Moscow's protection can assure that a reviving Germany won't demand them back.

It is a complicated scene. The Gomulka government has raised industrial wages and fought inflation pretty well lately, but Polish workers are still very poorly paid. It has sought to instill communism in Polish youth, but the young men and women of the universities are much more interested in job prospects and future salaries than in Marxist dialectics. It denounces Yugoslav behavior, but signs a trade agreement with Belgrade.

What is the equation here? Is it the Communist system versus the human spirit? Is it this, influenced also by that necessity for careful treading (with Moscow watching!) which persuaded Mr. Gomulka to refuse to see a Western journalist? Perhaps we can sum it all up by stating, in words which Mr. Gomulka might have chosen, what essentially is Poland's official role on the world stage today:

"Poland's first business is to survive! Remember that we lie between the Soviet Union and Soviet power as established in Eastern Germany. Hence the starting point of all our policy must be friendship with Moscow.

"Second, Poland must work steadily, hopefully, to reduce world tensions. Poland's freedom of action expands as world tensions subside—contracts as storm clouds gather and Moscow tightens up.

"That is why we have launched the Rapacki Plan—named after our foreign minister—to run a neutral, denuclearized zone right across the heart of Europe embracing Germany,

Poland, and Czechoslovakia. We think this plan could be the starting point of a general European pact.

"Third, Poland's role, as its rulers see it, is to be a Communist state—but a state that is operating by persuasion and patience rather than by secret police, and which takes local custom and tradition into consideration."

All right, Mr. Gomulka, and we'll just add that Poland is a laboratory where it is being demonstrated how the human spirit, the divine spark, over a long period will manifest itself in demands for freedom, in normal relations with the rest of mankind, and in a leavening of the dark mass of Marxist authoritarianism.

7

Tito

(YUGOSLAVIA)

Belgrade

THE STORY is told here that, when President Tito and Premier Khrushchev met at Brioni in September, 1956, to patch up the already crumbling Soviet-Yugoslav friendship arch, the Soviet premier demanded with homespun logic: "Josip, if one man in a platoon is out of step, how do you restore good marching order? Does the rest of the platoon change step or does this man get back in line?"

Shrewdly President Tito replied: "Nikita, it depends on what music the band is playing."

Yugoslavia's tough, unyielding leader has continued to insist all through his postwar relations with Moscow that he is following an authentic Marxist tune. It may not be the monolithic Soviet quickstep, but its tempo suits the south Slav temper. Today this tune has carried Yugoslavia down quite a different street from the avenue where the Soviet Union and its satellites are drilling.

It indeed can be said that because of Josip Broz Tito, and because of the sturdy-minded people of Yugoslavia, communism has historically acquired more than one definition. Despite all the fulminations of Moscow and Peking, there now are "several roads to socialism."

Government officials in Belgrade—and Marshal Tito himself—will readily explain Yugoslavia's separate course in foreign and domestic affairs to a visitor.

Just recently, it is pointed out, President Tito has been sailing his yacht *Galeb* along the coasts of Asia and the Middle East, preaching a "nonbloc" solidarity of middle-sized nations, eulogizing the virtues of uncommitted neutrality, building public sentiment for peaceful collaboration and public support for Yugoslavia—and profoundly annoying the Kremlin.

Just recently, also, Marshal Tito's Yugoslavia has been vaunting its style of communism, which is largely decentralized and stresses local control of industry and agriculture, with Workers' Councils—elected by factory workers—having a substantial voice in plant operations and salaries and sales policies, and with most of Yugoslavia's agriculture in the hands of small, uncollectivized peasant farmers.

This is some distance from Moscow's practice, which demands strict solidarity of the Communist bloc in foreign policy and which has decentralized operations but certainly not essential controls in the field of industry.

But let us ask President Tito to survey his policies in his own words. To the firm-jawed president with the iron-gray hair, I put the essential question asked of each world leader:

"What in your opinion is your country's essential role in today's world affairs?"

"Yugoslavia has consistently favored the right of every people to govern itself, and has favored noninterference in the internal affairs of other countries," he replied in writing. "This has earned Yugoslavia the full confidence of many nations, particularly in Asia and Africa."

Referring obviously to his own country and to the nations he has been visiting, the president continued: "The small and medium-sized countries have a very important role to play in the maintenance of peace—both in the United Nations and outside it—by taking a common stand on questions of vital significance."

The president indicated, as indeed one of his top ministers also had stressed in talking to me, that Yugoslavia's intention was to develop a "community of interest" among these uncommitted nations—a "collective conscience" of nonaligned peoples—which could mobilize sentiment toward the reduction of tensions and the halting of the cold war. President Tito has high regard for the persuasive power of world opinion.

"Material force is important, but moral force, which is imbuing the majority of mankind to a growing extent, has today become an even more powerful influence," he declared. "Should material force run counter to the strivings of the majority of mankind, it will suffer the same fate that befell the fascist coalition."

It is clear that Yugoslavia does not contemplate any formal alliance of uncommitted nations, any actual "nonbloc bloc." But officials here see no limits to this informal grouping of neutrals; they hope it will embrace not only India, Burma, Indonesia, and the United Arab Republic, for instance, but also such emergent nations as Ghana, Nigeria, and Guinea in Africa. They believe such a coalition of like-minded states could exert a potent force in the UN.

"We also support the Rapacki Plan [the deatomization and neutralization of Central Europe]," an official added. "Anything of this sort will force Moscow—and the West—to think and act less in terms of blocs."

It was obviously the purpose of President Tito's Afro-Asian voyage to build up the "community of interest" to which he has referred. It is also his purpose to circumvent Moscow's efforts to isolate him. He has most certainly avoided being isolated!

It is more difficult exactly to pinpoint Yugoslavia's domestic stance today—its domestic "road to socialism"—in that spectrum which ranges from Peking-brand communism through Khrushchevian-brand communism and on to socialism and capitalism.

Travel around Belgrade and out into the countryside, and one discovers signs of a loosening of heavy-handed controls—though the controls do remain in the background. At the turn of the year gaily lighted Christmas trees were allowed in the central squares for the first time. Also, there are more luxuries and amenities visible in the shop windows.

Downtown, in the first glow of evening, crowds stroll up and down certain boulevards, partially because it is a form of free entertainment. They display more jollity than heretofore. On New Year's Eve so many young revelers piled on the top of a passing American official's station wagon that they put quite a dent in the roof.

The growing amenities suggest that times are slowly getting better. Yugoslavia's industrialization program finally is beginning to pay off. Because there is now a plastics industry, plastic raincoats, umbrellas, and gadgets may be had. Because there is a machine-tool industry, officials hope to trade machinery and know-how eastward and bring back raw materials, citrus fruit, and other products from Asia and Africa.

"Our practice in the field of workers-management of factories and enterprises has yielded excellent results," President Tito comments. "We intend to continue along this path."

Yugoslavs call the Workers' Councils their "direct democracy." Certainly the elected factory councils do have a major hand in planning production, deciding on prices, and dividing profits. This is something unheard of in the Soviet Union, where a factory or mine is run by a government-appointed manager and the workers have virtually no say.

In some instances here the Workers' Councils have got out of hand, voting themselves (the workers and local management) bonuses of a half dozen extra "monthly incomes." The government has stepped in to recommend that two or three extra "monthly incomes" be the limit for one year.

The government also is building up the supposedly more zealous trade unions as a counterweight to the Workers' Councils. Theoretically, too, the factory director, nominated by the local parliament of the area, has veto rights. Finally, control is wielded by the financial powers of the government, which can grant or refuse loans for new factories, for expansion of old plants, for manufacture of new products.

The fact that Yugoslavia is marching along these other roads to socialism is treason in Moscow's eyes. But President Tito says: "After 1948 we ceased copying things not suited to our development [meaning Moscow's methods] and turned to the specific conditions of our own country."

Another Belgrade official puts it strikingly this way:

"Karl Marx was a man with a white beard who lived a century ago. Moscow, Peking, Belgrade, each claims to be following Marx; each cloaks its moves in ideological terms. Actually, he has little relevancy for today.

"It is foolhardy to try to prove who is 'Marxist.' The question today is: What system best mobilizes the country's energies?"

Because of this free wheeling, Peking in particular has lambasted Yugoslavia, subjecting its rulers to a choice selection of those ridiculous epithets which Communists are fond of hurling at one another—calling them "renegades," "Trotskyists," "revisionists," and "Trojan horses." I asked President Tito to comment on this.

"The bitter campaign of the Chinese Communists," he said, "cannot be explained in terms of the course Yugoslavia has elected in her efforts to build socialism, because this course is not a threat against the development of socialism in China or any other country."

In a speech at Novo Mesto in November, Marshal Tito spoke more sharply of the Chinese: "If they say they would not raise their living standards for fifteen more years because they want to build this and that, we could never have said this. Yugoslavia is working to improve the lot of people living today, not future generations."

In a rather unusual passage in another speech at Zrenjanin in November he declared: "Communists must in the first place be humanists. They must realize that they are the men who must serve their people. Yet, of what consists the happiness and the life of the people? This is something which I cannot measure myself, and therefore neither I nor anybody else can impose happiness on anyone. The people know of what their happiness consists, and this must be our guidance."

If we should take him at his word, President Tito is here enunciating something far different from the cold edicts of Peking or the strict Marxists—who perpetually contend that the State knows best and that service is owed by the people to the State.

One notes also that President Tito believes that Peking, in attacking Belgrade, also is hitting at Moscow and the mild Soviet strayings from the Stalinist "strait and narrow."

Marshal Tito thus finds himself billed as a considerable "revisionist." But we must not overweigh these evidences of a freer rein. Certainly Belgrade, compared with the satellite capitals, is a refreshing place. Yugoslavs, met most anywhere, are hearty, friendly people. Individually encountered in hotel lobby or government office, they step quickly over ideological barriers, and frequently will criticize, in private, governmental policy. (One also encounters in the streets of the capital that stolid gaze which reminds one that Yugoslavia is still largely a peasant nation.)

Despite the general friendliness, President Tito will permit no revisionism which would threaten his policies or conjure up an opposition party. For his repeated criticisms of the regime, Milovan Djilas languishes in jail. Several prewar trade-union and socialist leaders have been put on trial, and pro-Soviet sympathizers have been summarily rounded up. After long hesitation and despite obvious lingering misgivings, Marshal Tito approved the Soviet course in Hungary.

There is an American-style supermarket functioning here, purchased from the Americans after the Zagreb fair, where it was on display, but it is not privately owned. Except for the peasant farmers, there are few capitalists in Yugoslavia. The country is definitely not slowly "drifting into capitalism."

Belgrade churches are open, but sometimes young couples avoid church marriages so as to be more "eligible" for government jobs. Some automobiles are owned privately and some by factory organizations and other enterprises, but when the government recently criticized their "excessive" use for private errands and personal trips, cautious drivers dared hardly drive at all thereafter. Foreigners still are spied upon occasionally by the regime.

Nevertheless, here is another country, like Poland, which is not Marxist in the Muscovite sense. It is true that new "enterprising" is slowed and sometimes stifled because it all must funnel through state boards and government bureaucracy. President Tito's intention is still to build a Communist state, which means a state where the means of production are controlled by the government in the last analysis.

But if Marshal Tito is a dedicated Communist, he is no Stalinist. To be sure, the young Austro-Hungarian soldier of World War I, who was captured on the Eastern Front and was thus a prisoner of war in Russia at the cataclysmic moment when the revolution broke out, found his lifework and his loyalty in that encounter with history.

Specially trained in communism by Moscow, he later was returned to Yugoslavia, soon was jailed by the authorities for six years, then spent his time whipping discipline and effectiveness into the faction-rent Yugoslav Communist party. Reward came when World War II broke out, and Marshal Tito was able to build up a highly effective partisan army from the cadres he had organized.

As a result, Yugoslavia was able to free itself from the Nazis, at the close of World War II, with only minor help from Moscow. Hence Marshal Tito and his men never were beholden to the Soviet Union, and never had Soviet troops encamped in their midst. Hence when trouble fumed between the absolutist Stalin and independent-minded Tito, the Yugoslav chieftain did not have to knuckle under.

"I will lift my little finger," Stalin once said, "and there will be no more Tito." But the world is familiar with how Marshal Tito survived Stalin's finger lifting, and how later Mr. Khrushchev stood bareheaded at the Belgrade Airport in 1955 and apologized for Moscow's earlier mistreatment.

Premier Khrushchev, however, mistakenly believed that the split was merely a clash of personalities, and that warm words and welcoming embraces would bring back Marshal Tito into the fold. When Mr. Khrushchev could not swallow Marshal Tito's thesis of "separate roads" and when spreading "revisionism" in Hungary and Poland threatened to get out of hand, Moscow again demanded that Yugoslavia pledge full subservience to the Soviet Union's authority and infallibility.

This Marshal Tito refused, as might have been anticipated from past performance. And so once again he is an outcast from the Soviet camp, although occasionally Mr. Khrushchev tosses a not unfriendly word in his direction.

So Marshal Tito has survived—he of the determined mien, the resilient mind, and the watchful light-blue eyes. Besides being a Communist and a tough partisan, acquaintances find him a very human individual, with an attractive sense of humor and a disarming pleasure in good living—and even in bright uniforms.

President Tito's greatest fault, in the eyes of Moscow, is that he is experimenting with new roads, new forms of socialism. In a sense this means—in these days when ideas pack vast power—that little Yugoslavia is really on the offensive and that the Soviet-Chinese monolith is on the defensive. As the human spirit thus roams more freely, who can say where this eventually will lead the sturdy Yugoslavs?

8

Bourguiba

(TUNISIA)

Tunis

NORTH AFRICA! The very words conjure the vision of white-walled coastal cities, farmlands stretching south toward the Sahara, native casbahs, Hannibal and Hasdrubal of ancient Carthage, and the granaries of the Roman Empire.

President Bourguiba of Tunisia has a great dream for this vast area—for these modern cities of Tunis, Algiers, Oran, Casablanca; for the backward farmlands and modern settlements; for Morocco, Algeria, Tunisia, perhaps Libya.

It is the dream of a North African federation embracing these countries—perhaps a confederation, perhaps a single state.

In an Africa which is in a ferment of freedom seeking, President Bourguiba's conception is most significant. For his North African federation or state would not be an alien, West-shunning, "anti-imperialist" concoction, breathing fire and brimstone on the former "colonial powers."

Rather does French-educated, Gallic-mannered, West-admiring Habib Bourguiba—an Arab Charles Boyer in appearance—favor close ties with France and with the West. Indeed, he has even a larger goal ahead: to bring together the major countries on both shores of the Mediterranean—France, Italy, Spain, Tunisia, Algeria, Morocco, perhaps others—into a political-economic association.

Where other men have talked of "Atlantic Union," Bourguiba envisions "Mediterranean Basin."

Tunisia is the size of Louisiana. Its population is about four million. The president sees small Tunisia's large role in world affairs as a dedication to this regional development—stabilizing North Africa, uniting it, maintaining its old allegiances despite the rising tide of pan-Arabism and the perils of a prolonged Algerian war, which could wreck everything and open the doors to communism.

Great danger threatens the dream of this dynamic, effervescent Tunisian, as he sees it. It is the peril of France's desperate effort to hold Algeria, next door to him. If this war continues, Mr. Bourguiba fears that France's relations with North Africa will be demolished for a generation. An uncompromising, onsweeping North African "nationalism" will build, which will spoil all plans for constructive solutions.

But let us interview President Bourguiba in his home on the Riviera-like Mediterranean slope outside Tunis and hear his own words on these portentous subjects.

Somehow, as we approach on the winding road between the well-kept villas, the whole area breathes "North Africa." The near-by hills are dotted with remnants of Roman Carthage, and Hannibal's Carthage before it. A Roman aqueduct marches in broken step; there are ancient cisterns, pillars, and statue fragments in the local gardens; sections of pictured mosaic flooring are being constantly unearthed.

Today, French culture has been infused here, overlaying

that of Turk, Berber, Levantine, and Arab. Past the guards at Mr. Bourguiba's door, we are ushered into a sun-filled room of many windows. Outside, the blue sea stretches into the Mediterranean distances. Inside, there are beige hangings, furniture of unbleached wood, a dramatic bookcase, a white rug, a large desk. There is nothing drab in this office.

With attendant officials, there are five of us besides the president, but he might have been addressing an audience of five hundred, considering the drama of gesturing hands, arms, shoulders, and expressive eyes. He has an arresting platform presence. I cannot follow his rapid French, but I am totally fascinated—as must be the Tunisian crowds who surge to hear him as he speaks, with rarely a prepared text.

Every small, emergent country seems to need a leader—someone in whom public trust can repose. Habib Bourguiba is that, and because Tunisia has been freed, and because he insists on being a special, unsolicited North African adviser to the French, he can do much to influence the crucial solutions in North Africa. It is not every day that an indigenous champion in these parts is openly pro-Western, enthusiastically pro-American.

But Mr. Bourguiba—considering the temper of his own people, newly emerged from colonialism—cannot continue in this orientation if the West merely takes him for granted. Let us hear his argument.

"It is extremely important," he says, spreading out his hands, palms up, "that Tunisia is one of the few countries that has torn itself loose from France and is still maintaining good relations with France. Tunisia can serve as an example, if events permit this.

"I want to develop among the Tunisian people the conviction that progress and prosperity are the direct fruits of co-operation with other countries. Tunisia cannot live alone. That is why we are glad to cooperate with the West.

"Now the West in turn, by helping to ensure prosperity in North Africa, can prove to all the world that when a colonial people attains its freedom it can remain the friend of the former colonial power. But if—as with France presently in Algeria—you give a people unasked-for solutions and fail to satisfy their aspirations, the result is catastrophic."

President Bourguiba has experienced imprisonment and exile at the hands of France. He returned triumphantly to Tunisia in June, 1955, when the Franco-Tunisian Conventions were signed giving Tunisia internal autonomy. He thereupon rebuilt the Neo-Destour (New Constitution) party which he had founded in 1934. In April, 1956, after many clashes with Paris and hesitations on the part of Paris, Tunisian independence was allowed and President Bourguiba formed the first government of independent Tunisia. In July, 1957, a republic was proclaimed.

France had freed Tunisia and Morocco but retained Algeria, claiming that this is an integral part of metropolitan France.

"If the Algerian war continues four to five years more, then no one can attain a prosperous and secure settlement there—just as was the case in Indo-China," the president comments. Rightly or wrongly convinced of this, he feels that Tunisia must keep pressing France for a favorable solution—and must simultaneously line up its neighbors in the common North African front.

"The unity of the Maghreb area was a historical fact in antiquity," he reminds. "In the age of colonial acquisitions we became separated. It will take time to forge a real unity, but we must work in that direction.

"The pace and the outcome will depend so very much on France, and on what happens in these very next years. If Morocco leans toward Nasser—and there are signs of such a trend—and if Algeria, in desperation, seeks the aid of the Communists, it will be impossible to realize any sort of North African unity.

"Look at India. If India had had to fight the British in a long, hard struggle, I wonder if Nehru would be there today; certainly India would not have the kind of government that it now has.

"That is why we have pushed the French to deal with Algeria as she has dealt with Tunisia and Morocco. We have told the French that if they reach a peaceful arrangement, they can facilitate a North African union, and be associated with this union."

The president, directly addressing me, continued:

"And that is why we ask our American friends to push France in the same manner."

Mr. Bourguiba had made an oblique reference to President Nasser of the United Arab Republic. He had broken off diplomatic relations with Cairo, charging Nasser-inspired attempts to assassinate him. I asked the president to outline his attitude toward Egypt.

"Being an Arab people, with the same language, we have felt close to the Middle Eastern countries," he replied. "But we have had difficulties. It is mainly that President Nasser has been trying—as the French are trying in Algeria—to impose a certain kind of domination throughout the area.

"We have had to fight these things with the same determination as we fought foreign domination. We have kept this influence in check." (He gestured sharply as he spoke the French word "échec.")

"I believe that in taking this stand, full of dignity, we are helping the Middle Eastern peoples to realize their real interests. Our stand has been the cause in part of certain Cairo defeats—as in its efforts to establish dominion over Lebanon and the Sudan.

"Tunisia will continue to play this role effectively unless certain Western countries help Nasser to reinforce his policies in the Middle East," he added warningly.

Mr. Bourguiba is one of the few men in this part of the world who have stood up to President Nasser, and he did not flirt with Communist support as did Brigadier Abdel Karim el-Kassem in Iraq. Though backed by only a small country, he is engaged in a veritable tug of war with Cairo to determine whether North Africa shall be pulled toward Egypt or shall build its own future.

Within the past months, the president has shifted his pro-Western stance slightly. When it seemed that the United States and Britain would not sell arms to Tunisia without French "approval," he said he would be forced to look for armaments wherever he could find them, be it in Germany, Turkey, or Czechoslovakia.

"If the West supports colonial forces—and here I mean France—I cannot be an accomplice to this sort of thing, before my people.

"Of course," the president added, "if the United States dissociates itself from French policy in Algeria, or can draw France away from its present policy, then I will reapproach my former position."

President Bourguiba said he did not think that French President de Gaulle was yet proposing anything in the way of a realistic solution for Algeria.

Obviously Tunisia's influence will be impressive to the degree that it succeeds in becoming a prosperous, well-governed nation. It was not surprising then that President Bourguiba—who had just completed a speech-making, ear-to-the-ground tour of his southern domains—should respond as he did when I asked him what seemed to be the most encouraging domestic development in Tunisia today.

"It is," he replied, opening wide his arms, "that we have been developing so well, so solidly, our independence. I have seen independence taking form in concrete results, day by day.

"I remember how in the first months of our freedom we had to face heavy problems. We had to counter French demands; we had to take command of our own troops, set up a police force. We had to find suitable officials, a civil service. We set up banks, a foreign office; we saw to it that France, however unwillingly, evacuated its troops."

French forces in Tunisia are now confined to the naval base at Bizerte, and the president would like to see this transformed into a base "held for the use of the North Atlantic Treaty Organization."

"History shows that people who have confidence in themselves, as we have, inspire the confidence of others toward them," he said proudly.

"What is the biggest domestic challenge that you face?" I asked.

"Security remains a problem. The French Army is on our border, in its Algerian struggle. The danger here does not come from the government of France, but from what the military people in Algeria might still do, going beyond instructions from Paris."

With President de Gaulle in power, such insubordination may not happen again, of course.

"Another great challenge is to carry through with the emancipation of Tunisian women. We have made significant progress. The education of future generations depends on the enlightenment of the women of Tunisia."

Here, significantly, President Bourguiba, leader of a Moslem nation, was taking the same stand as Prime Minister Jawaharlal Nehru, the leader of Hindu India. Both were declaring that a great necessity of these twentieth-century years was to lift the mental and physical bondage from womankind in their lands.

At some of his rallies throughout the country, President Bourguiba will have a veiled Tunisian woman come to the platform—many still go veiled, even on the wide, French-designed boulevards of modern Tunis, the capital city. Then he will gently remove that white, masking veil, explaining the symbolism of what he is doing. Staged or not, it is very impressive. Even in the less advanced south, one finds branches of the Union National des Femmes de Tunisie, which is working to establish equal rights and customs for women.

"We must also expand the standard of living of the Tunisian people," he adds. "That is a great challenge."

The United States contributed 20 million dollars last year in foreign aid. Tunisia requires twice that amount from abroad, at present, to keep afloat economically. Economic assistance is also coming from France. In the past twenty-five years Tunisia's population has increased by 60 per cent, while production rose only 25 per cent.

Americans here have suggested that Tunisia be made a showcase of what democratic upbuilding can accomplish; but there are many demands on American aid in all parts of the world. More tourism can be promoted along Tunisia's coast line, with its handsome beaches, good climate, and ancient ruins. Efforts are being made, with American aid, to improve agriculture, modernize the pottery industry, introduce banana growing.

President Bourguiba, alert to public trends, makes a weekly broadcast to the nation, which is a very effective piece of public enlightenment and personal politicking. He is a little concerned about the youth of Tunisia, who listen to the Cairo radio and sign anticolonial declarations when visiting or studying abroad. He has recently taken student groups behind closed doors and explained his policies to them. He convinced quite a few.

Rather remarkably, to sum it all up, here is an Arab leader whose natural inclination is to maintain close ties with the West. The West, in view of the tremendous stakes in awakened Africa, should do everything that it honorably can to enable this bouncy, resourceful North African to hold to his course, with favoring Mediterranean winds.

9

Nasser

(EGYPT)

Cairo

GAMAL ABDEL NASSER urged upon me, in our interview, that the prime mission of the United Arab Republic in today's world is to help hurry the nations of the Middle East—and indeed the whole Afro-Asian multitude—past that period of instability, envy, and frustration which he describes as "the most dangerous condition confronting the world."

Yes, to hurry these nations—by leadership, inspiration, joint action—past their undeveloped stages and on into better, saner, calmer standards of living.

This, President Nasser maintained—sitting at ease on a plain sofa in the workroom of his unpretentious villa in a Cairo suburb—is the end and aim of his interventions in Middle Eastern affairs which have so alarmed some countries.

"The Middle East, recently dominated by colonial powers, was a vacuum," he explained. "There were no ideas, no common bonds, no national feelings. Egypt's role has not been to force a spurious unity on the region; that would have been colonialism in a new form. But people live by ideas. I have sought to develop an ideology of Arab nationalism to fill the vacuum."

How well he succeeded was widely evident in the portraits of Mr. Nasser which smiled from the walls of Damascus, the bazaars of Baghdad, and even the *souks* of Tunis.

But Mr. Nasser's popularity has been challenged by a military change-over in the Sudan, by Jordan's "no-surrender" King Hussein, and most recently and joltingly by communism's open and defiant penetration of the Iraqian regime of Brigadier Abdel Karim el-Kassem.

President Nasser is always devoid of bombast, always reasonable in an interview, I was told in Egypt. Whether this is true in every instance I cannot say. But I can say that he —and Egyptian officialdom generally—seemed particularly friendly and thoughtful at this time, as though revising some of their own outlook and strategy. The chill frost sifting down from the Kremlin towers was certainly a contributing cause.

I admit to receiving a favorable, sympathetic view of President Nasser as he stepped from behind a desk piled high with papers to greet me modestly and as he genially posed for photographs beside the flowered borders inside his guarded walls. I had just come from seeing examples of the progress Egypt has made in building new technical schools, improving poultry breeding, and launching its industrial base. Nasser is the grand vizier of this progress; to Egyptians and to many beyond the borders of his country he is the hero of the bright new day.

There is of course another side to the United Arab Republic regime. There is the Voice of the Arabs radio and its broadcasts, speaking diatribes against all who oppose Cairo's designs and calling for the assassination of King Hussein of Jordan. There are the Egyptian schoolteachers who carry, along with modern learning, indoctrination in Cairo's point of view to pupils all the way from Saudi Arabia to Morocco. There are the Egyptian military attachés who have been expelled for allegedly sowing unrest in neighboring armies.

But let us hear from President Nasser himself. The first question is: "What achievement in today's Egypt are you the proudest of?"

"It is easy to build dams," Mr. Nasser replies. "It is more difficult to build people. My greatest achievement is the confidence which the Egyptian people have in themselves and in Egypt and in their future.

"Morale is of greatest importance. During the Suez aggression in 1956, it became clear what had been accomplished. I went down into the country, and I found confidence, I found dignity.

"Our people previously had been affected by each small incident, by each street-corner demonstration. Now they are sure of themselves, matured. They are not as emotional as they were."

President Nasser did not say so, but obviously that confidence to a large degree rests on himself, for he is, in the public eye, the man who by some magic managed to frustrate the Suez intentions of the French, British, and Israelis, who has made the Suez Canal a successful source of revenue (and how needed!), and who has even managed to obtain and retain Soviet assistance in reviving the High Dam project near Aswan.

I asked him to expand further on this peril of instability among the underdeveloped nations, to which he had alluded.

"The world is small today compared with twenty years ago," he replied. "Any villager can know of the United States or the Soviet Union. He can compare his lot with that of others.

"But, do you know, people are not jealous so much as they are ambitious. They simply want to improve their living standards, to catch up—yes, to catch up by any means! We pay too much attention to the cold war, and not enough to the problems and tensions of the newly developing nations.

"For instance, people are looking at Communist China. Africa particularly is watching China's progress, wondering if it should adopt China's Communist methods. The Indians are studying this, too."

"Do you feel that Egypt should adopt the police-state methods employed in mainland China?" I asked.

"No, we in Egypt have got beyond that stage of organization. Communism should have no appeal here. But we must remember there can be no neutrality between development and underdevelopment. Things need to be done."

Some economists are not certain that Egypt, even with all its rural reform and high resolve, has yet got safely beyond the danger point—beyond the point where the new industrial base can begin to raise living standards faster than the crowding birth rate depresses them.

Even when the Aswan High Dam is completed, bringing 2 million more acres into cultivation, there will be by then five million more people to feed. Yet Egypt most certainly presents the appearance today of a nation on the move, its leadership in the hands of a determined group of men.

Meanwhile, President Nasser has jailed, or tossed into a desert concentration camp, all troublesome domestic Communists. Reared as a boy in an Egyptian village—in Assiut

Province of Upper Egypt—he has a peasant regard for the land and believes that the *fellahin* should own their Nile-irrigated acres—no communes for him!

"We have directed all our effort toward freedom—and productivity," he continued. "Freedom is not sufficient to produce stability. A people must have confidence in their future prospects, confidence that there will be equality of opportunity and certainty of a job, and no avaricious landlords and moneylenders. Your democratic system promises freedom; it must also promise equality of opportunity—and jobs.

"Peace is not only a question of external aggression, but also of internal stability. A few small countries can upset world peace if they lack internal stability. Take Iraq, for instance. Iraq's people need to be sure that their government is working for them. They have been unsure—as our own people here were uncertain in the first months after our revolution. Now our people are assured."

President Nasser's comments suggest that he may again, after a period of concentration on affairs beyond his borders, be coming to grips with those obstacles which any new country must face after the departure of the foreign troops: the raw, stark needs in the shape of loans, credits, blueprints. Egypt, though large on the maps, is a poor country, the Nile valley its only fertile area. Cairo is a showplace but its villages are shabby collections of mud huts.

"You see," Mr. Nasser commented, "we missed the age of steam, the dawn of electricity. Now it is the age of the atom and we must work doubly hard to catch up. So we need a plan of action. Actually, for development programs we need two things: manpower, of which we have a surplus, and investment funds and technical knowledge, of which we can never have too much."

"What are your terms and conditions today for accepting foreign aid?" I asked him, noting that he had bought armaments from the Soviet Union and Czechoslovakia, paying for them with a portion of Egypt's cotton crop over a period of five years. "There are apprehensions in the West that this course of action—plus acceptance of Soviet economic aid—has put you irretrievably in the Soviet camp," I added.

"The condition under which we take foreign aid," he commented, "is simply this: no political ties. Of course we like to have low rates of interest and a long time to pay off. The Soviet Union gave us a loan at 2½ per cent and twelve years to pay—after the factory has been built and is producing. We will, however, accept less favorable terms—we already have from Japan and West Germany. But the main point is not to mix development with politics.

"Now if Soviet assistance helps me to build a stronger Egypt, then that will enable me to be stronger to avoid the 'strings' which might be attached. And the more productive and prosperous our country is made to be, through foreign assistance, the less appeal communism will have in Egypt."

Some people have indeed felt that President Nasser is more interested in foreign intrigue and in amassing a large empire than in improving things at home in Egypt, I said. For instance, some had taken alarm at the wide range of his ambitions, as seemingly revealed in his book, *Philosophy of Revolution*.

"That book was written in 1953," President Nasser replied, adding with a laugh: "After the hue and cry it raised, I decided to write no more books. But have you actually read the book, or just heard what someone said about it?"

He went to a shelf and picked up a copy to show me, but it turned out to be a version in Arabic.

"When I was teaching in our staff college, I delved into the problems of the Mediterranean basin," he continued. "History, I found, showed quite naturally that when the Arab countries were united they rid themselves of invaders.

"From this reading of history I saw that those things which should have been our strengths, such as our geographical position, or the oil of the area, were used as justifications for occupying us. Instead, they should have been sources of strength and protection to us.

"So I began first by working to build an Arab nationalism which would apply to all the Middle East. A vacuum had to be filled, as I've said. Egypt in the Middle East is not playing the role of an invader, but as a supplier of ideas.

"Ideas have power. Militarily, today, a big power could bring 100,000 troops and occupy us. But if we are imbued with Arab nationalism, those who would invade us must think many times. The invader would need a million men to conquer Egypt today."

"Do the other Arab countries agree with your estimate of the situation, your sense of mission?" I asked.

"Having seen all of these countries, I can conclude that all are feeling basically similar. All want full political independence. All want social and economic development. The threats against all of us have produced more of a desire for solidarity. Of course, unity of the Arab world is not something novel. It existed in the eleventh century."

I remarked to the president that he had made a sizable impression on many of the Bandung Conference nations. Did his interest extend beyond the Arab world? Was he working to promote Afro-Asian solidarity?

"There are different spheres of interest to be considered," he answered. "First is our own progress and development. Second is the cause of freedom in the Arab world. Third is the necessity for freedom and development throughout the Afro-Asian world. Of course we are interested in all of these.

"It is vital to practice coexistence. To us this also means nonalignment—no supporting of one power bloc against another. Many nations feel this way."

Turning to a wholly new topic, I asked President Nasser about his terms for peace with Israel. Suppose Israel gave proof that it was not expansionist bent and showed greater flexibility on the frontier issue. Could a stable peace be developed?

"Really we do not think of the solution that way," he quickly answered. "The big problem to us is the million refugees who were expelled from Palestine and replaced by other people. How can this be accepted? The main question is the rights of these refugees."

Should there be a plebiscite to determine who wished to return home, and who would be willing, if compensated, to settle in other Arab territories? I asked.

"If I were a refugee I would want to return to my home. We Arabs are a sentimental people.

"The second problem is the philosophy of Israel. In their election campaign a few years ago the Israelis talked of extending their sway from the Nile to the Euphrates. This created a threat to Egypt, Syria, Jordan, Lebanon, Iraq. This led to our policy of buying arms. What was the use of building schools, if the Israelis were to occupy those schools?

"I have never said we should 'drive Israel into the sea.' But these questions must be settled satisfactorily."

Bluntly I said that he had been accused of seeking to extend his sway over the oil "have" nations. What was his reply to this?

"If I said I wanted to control the oil of the Middle East, they'd all be against me," he laughed. "Actually we intend to increase our own oil production. We have three fields here now, one in Syria. By 1960 I am in hopes that we shall be self-sufficient in oil."

This, then, is President Nasser, who has landed on his feet after a good many apparent reverses and who now must contend with the prospect that Moscow expects him to accept the direct intrusion of Communist party power into his domain—and to grin and bear it.

Eventually the Middle East is likely to attain some kind of unity, federation at least. How peacefully this is accomplished, whether Communist internationalism is thwarted in its Middle East bid, and how diligently the new dynamism of the area is channeled into improvements in its own back yard—more irrigation, more schools, more agricultural reform, more basic industries—may depend in no small degree on this agile gentleman from the banks of the Nile and how he uses his brilliantly seized opportunities.

10

Nkrumah

(GHANA)

Accra

DARK-SKINNED AFRICA is formidably, enthusiastically on the march toward independence, and Ghana's prime minister, Kwame Nkrumah, is leading the parade. Is this youthful, impulsive, "likes-to-be-liked" African—now ruling where once the first European traders built their castlelike coastal forts—destined to be the Talleyrand who can merge disparate former colonies into a United States of Africa?

Or will the leadership be wrenched away by a tougher candidate such as Guinea's Sekou Touré, whose socialism is more Marxist, or by a prime minister from a larger commonwealth, such as emerging Nigeria?

Or will they all fail, as Simon Bolívar failed in South America? Will "African Africa" remain ununited because its tribal differences, its lack of trade ties, and its geographical Balkanization are too difficult to overcome?

"The people in West Africa are ready for unity; there is a ground swell of support for federation all through the area," confidently declares Prime Minister Nkrumah.

Let us visit Ghana's prime minister here in Christiansborg

Castle, once a Danish fort and for long years the residence of the British governor of the Gold Coast. Let us climb to his breeze-swept office high on the castle walls, above the surf which rolls ceaselessly across the warm sands fronting harborless Accra.

Here is the African, educated in the United States at Lincoln University and in Britain, who to a degree symbolizes those factors which have put little Ghana (population five million, area the size of Britain) ahead in Africa's surprising independence race.

For Ghana—formerly the Gold Coast—was for years a "model colony" of Britain's. Young men found scholarships for study abroad. The profitable cocoa trade (Ghana produces one-half of the world's cocoa crop) has made it wealthy by African standards. More than a few Accra families have sent their sons and daughters to British universities.

The old traders and gold miners early needed African clerks and helpers; hence literacy has been somewhat higher here than in neighboring colonies. The British colonial system was more enlightened—trained more civil servants—than the French did in Guinea or the Belgians in the Congo. There is, also, more homogeneity in Ghana than in near-by British-ruled Nigeria (gaining independence in 1960), where 250 tribes speak a myriad languages.

The quick visitor to Ghana early discovers a land where the color bar—openly present in the American South, subtly present in the American North and in much of Europe—is actually absent. Europeans, Americans, Indians, and Africans mingle without race consciousness, whether at diplomatic receptions, in hotel dining rooms, or in the night clubs where people dance to "high-life" music, an African jazz which is brother under the brown skin to West Indian calypso.

Obviously, racial discrimination would have short shrift in a proud new African nation where the power resides—and make no mistake—in the hands of its native people.

There is a zest in the air, as of independence so recently achieved. Freedom is a heady concoction. Parliament sits with less decorum than in England. Mr. Nkrumah's picture is unabashedly on stamps and coins. People cheer emissaries of the ruling Congress People's party, crowd into their election rallies. Newspapers talk of big construction projects.

And careful foreign observers warn that some highly placed officials around Mr. Nkrumah have accepted more than a "normal" share of "squeeze" from the new development contracts—more than any city political boss in the United States would regard as his rightful graft. Ostentatious new wealth is visible here and there.

Meanwhile the opposition party in Parliament has been reduced to a pitiful few, and is poorly led and inadequately financed, though embracing some of Ghana's ablest conservative lawyers and merchants. Undoubtedly it has concocted unworthy and irresponsible schemes to influence the public; at the same time Mr. Nkrumah's Congress People's party has kept the opposition throttled by overwhelming election victories and occasional strong-arm threats.

Is this the "mud-bath period" of a bold new venture? Or is a pattern of one-party rule and strong-arm government setting in willy-nilly? Can a new nation move any faster in developing responsible parliamentary democracy when there are wide differences of wealth and literacy between the city-bred few and the vast multitude of the hinterland and when the old tribal order changeth slowly?

"In my thirty years here the Gold Coast has never had a more stable regime," declares a veteran European. "Parliamentary government is not learned overnight."

But the appointment with the prime minister is now ready. I enter a large, airy office, replete with mementos of Mr. Nkrumah's visits to neighboring lands and to India—reminders of his foreign policy: a lovely reproduction of the Taj Mahal done in ivory, signed photographs from Indian Prime Minister Jawaharlal Nehru, and a model of the first freighter to sail under the Ghana flag.

Mr. Nkrumah steps forward to greet me, an average-sized figure in a blue business suit. He says that, if he had expected photographs would be taken, he would have worn the blue-striped northern territory "smock" which he wears frequently in Parliament.

The prime minister is a man with quick, intelligent eyes beneath a high forehead—an individual who, we have been told, could on occasion be dramatic, as before a cheering crowd, or statesmanlike, as when conferring with Mr. Nehru, or insecure, as when being told of a "plot" against him by some scheming subordinate, or impulsive.

I had glimpsed the more delightful side of impulsiveness the previous day at the formal parliamentary ceremonies accepting the gift of a new "Speaker's chair" from the British House of Commons.

As the ceremonies neared their solemn climax, Mr. Nkrumah leaped up, called on his front benchers, clad in their bright *kente* cloths, to follow him, and strode to where the chair was waiting. Together the majority party members lifted it up, carried it shoulder high to where the widely respected Speaker was waiting, and plumped him into it.

A job ordained for the sober-suited Parliament ushers had been done by the members of Parliament themselves—and everyone laughed, cheered, and was delighted.

As we sat down in his office I put to Prime Minister Nkrumah the fundamental question: "How do you see Ghana's role in world affairs or African affairs today?"

"I believe in African unity," he replied. "I believe that Ghana should be united in a very close association with the rest of West Africa—beginning with near-by Guinea, with which we have already arranged steps toward merger.

"With Guinea, the former French colony, we hope to set up a common currency, a single national defense, and one flag. The general public supports this. Throughout West Africa there is a ground swell of support for acting together.

"Ultimately, yes, I would think a 'United States of Africa' might result. But the association in West Africa can be even closer, perhaps a single nation eventually. Today's boundaries are artificial, set up without rhyme or reason by the colonial powers."

The prime minister was careful not to project himself as the sole prime mover toward West African unification. Recently President Tubman of Liberia and Leopold-Sedar Senghor of Senegal have shown resentment at the way Mr. Nkrumah has seized the ball and run with it.

"This West African development has got to be a cooperative undertaking," he said. "We have to get rid of the remaining ties of colonialism."

Prime Minister Nkrumah is aware that France is not keen to see its African colonies tying up with former British possessions which now or soon will be members of the British Commonwealth. He is aware also that African leaders in the French colonies—including perhaps even Guinea—may be inclined to string along for a while with France so long as France invests sufficient francs in local development programs.

But the prime minister, drawing on his own experience in Ghana, which had indeed been a "model" British colony, believes that the surge for freedom will overwhelm economic instincts in the long run.

He also argues that there is a big difference between the new French "community" proposed by President de Gaulle and the Commonwealth association of nations to which his Ghana belongs.

The French "community" is undoubtedly a break with the old French concept of building a native elite (composed of officials educated in Paris) who should rule the colony. But there is still a deep suspicion in Africa that the new French "community" will not present to the former colonies anything like absolute freedom.

The British have done it astutely. Ghana, though entirely free, remains within the Commonwealth. And, strangely enough, there now are more Europeans, mainly British, in Ghana than before independence. Then they were government civil servants; today a few are still governmental advisers; the remainder are contractors, engineers, merchants, salesmen, entrepreneurs.

In short—and here is a lesson for all colonial powers—Ghana is more valuable to Britain today as a Commonwealth partner and a member of the sterling area than it was as a closely held colony.

But Ghana is not preoccupied with foreign affairs. The

public expected great things to flow from independence—literacy, better housing, plenty of jobs. Prime Minister Nkrumah feels he has to produce. Some projects are moving along well. In a few hours the visitor can see the new harbor and town being constructed at Tema, twenty miles from Accra; can marvel at the new university buildings rising just outside the capital; can visit the green-uniformed work brigades—modeled after the United States Civilian Conservation Corps of the 1930's—which are providing artisan training to some of Ghana's unemployed.

"What is the most encouraging development now under way inside Ghana?" I asked the prime minister.

"My answer may be considered naïve," he replied, "but I believe it is the mass education, the community development, the whole effort we are making to raise the intelligence level of our citizenry.

"I refer to the new schools we have built, to the buildings added to our university, to community programs. We are fighting not only disease, not only illiteracy, but the ignorance which has long beset Africa."

These seemed excellent goals, corroborating the view expressed by close observers that the prime minister is an idealistic man of considerable integrity, though often subject to ill-considered advice from certain members of his inner entourage.

I asked the prime minister whether he believed that Ghana, as a new state, was ready for parliamentary government or whether it would have to fall back on some kind of authoritarianism, as had Pakistan and the Sudan.

Two opposition leaders have been on trial, charged with seeking to bribe a small contingent of police to "arrest" the prime minister at the airport when he embarked for India. Fantastically, the bribe fund totaled only 50 pounds ($125). Some thirty-eight other opposition members have been held in jail under the Preventive Detention Act.

"We want an opposition party," Mr. Nkrumah answered. "It's always better to have opposition outside the government rather than inside it. But our opponents of today are badly led. They should operate as a loyal opposition, along constitutional lines. They should have a program with which to appeal to the electorate instead of dealing in dark plots against the government.

"The opposition needs to learn patience. In time the wheel swings round. Look at Canada and how the Conservatives suddenly became the dominant party.

"Nobody is going to liquidate the opposition in Parliament," he assured. "Meanwhile we want to improve our Constitution so as to maintain a strong Parliament."

Some British and European experts in Ghana, however, believe that it will evolve more and more into a one-party state. Indeed, perhaps this is the inevitable present destiny of most of the newly emerging states of West Africa: Senegal, Upper Volta, Guinea, Dahomey. These countries, sprung from tribal society, have no tradition of able dissent, no appreciation for a "loyal opposition." It is felt, too, that educated citizens are too few in number to be spread around in competing parties.

Opposition parties, usually representing regional instead of national interests, are not really able to win national election contests. As in Ghana, they tend to attack everything the government does, almost by force of habit, and hence discredit themselves.

In the earlier tribal societies, people spoke their mind on a local issue, a decision (often a compromise) was reached, and then dissent and opposition ended. In former French Guinea there is today a single national party, composed of thousands of village committees or councils. Perhaps this is closer to the African's experience and will work better, at least at present. Certainly two-party government is not now functioning efficiently in Ghana. Nigeria may show a different result; it has three main parties of some strength. Its big, forty-million population may be able to enjoy multiparty democracy for quite a period.

Prime Minister Nkrumah doesn't really need to use the sledgehammer blows which he has been meting out to the opposition party, even if some opponents have indeed engaged in fantastic plottings. His conduct makes sense only if one considers that he is engaged in developing a very strong "home base," so that he may safely leave Ghana from time to time to sell his unification ideas to neighboring states and territories.

Opponents charge that the Nkrumah regime, relying on the doctrine of "parliamentary supremacy," is prepared to impair the integrity of the law courts. Recently Parliament rushed through a bill which exonerated a former Cabinet member and a police commissioner from contempt of court charges, thus interfering with judicial process.

"We shall probably make Ghana a republic before long, but remain within the Commonwealth, as is India. I am not sure whether our ultimate form of government should include both a prime minister and a president or a president combining both the ceremonial and executive functions," Mr. Nkrumah continued.

"What we must indeed preserve are these three features:

universal adult suffrage, freedom for anybody to form a political party, and periodic general elections. These are the essentials."

I asked the prime minister about his new five-year development program. Some 80 million pounds was expended under the first plan; now a new program is contemplated, to cost between 240 and 300 million pounds.

"We must move ahead with programs to diversify our agriculture, to add industry," he said. "The Volta River project, providing a tremendous hydroelectric dam supplying current to be used for manufacturing aluminum from our vast bauxite deposits, is a first priority. Obviously, we cannot provide all the funding for this. We would accept foreign aid for such a program."

This, then, is the new state of Ghana—where women, dressed in exotic prints, walk gracefully erect, balancing huge water cans and market baskets on their heads; where members of Parliament and other dignitaries wear their heavy native-woven *kente*-cloth robes in the manner of Roman togas; where, upcountry, the old chieftain rule is being upset by the new Nkrumah party; where cocoa is grown on thousands of small farms, producing a revenue almost as rich per capita as the oil royalties paid to Middle East kingdoms.

Undoubtedly graft is prevalent at some government levels. Yet there are favorable factors, too. Foremost is the fact that Mr. Nkrumah's Cabinet is drawn not from the conservative "elite" of Ghana but, as one observer put it, "right off the mob."

This means that communism isn't finding it easy to gain a foothold in Ghana. The Nkrumah regime represents most directly the man in the street, and the prime minister understands his hopes and desires.

Obviously, Mr. Nkrumah is not intending to relinquish the leadership in Africa's freedom surge which he has so far maintained. West African events may overthrow him, of course. Or a long-term failure to make Ghana blossom according to election promises may unseat him.

So far, though, he is doing pretty well. And certainly, among the list of choices, it is hopeful that the front runner today is a product of American education and British parliamentary tutelage and a politician who, however impulsive he may be at times, does believe basically in the equality of man.

But there will be other candidates soon—other prime ministers and officials to challenge Kwame Nkrumah for the role of Pan-African leadership. And some of these, such as Dr. Hastings Banda of Nyasaland, Tom Mboya of Kenya, Obafemi Awolowo and "Zik" Azikiwe of Nigeria, and Sekou Touré of Guinea could be formidable competitors indeed.

11

Ben-Gurion

(ISRAEL)

Tel Aviv

ISRAEL IS a pilot plant for mankind. In compact phrase this expresses Prime Minister David Ben-Gurion's conception of his small country's special contribution to humanity, its potential role in world affairs.

A pilot plant—a test laboratory or first workshop—what exactly did he mean? I asked the short, powerfully built man, whose weathered face and halo of white hair gave him a patriarchal mien as we sat together in his unpretentious Ministry of Defense office.

Mr. Ben-Gurion today exemplifies the state of Israel. When he rolls up his sleeves to work in a Negev desert settlement, Israeli youth is powerfully moved to follow his example. When he addresses Parliament, the Army, or Histradut, the potent labor organization, his countrymen listen with deepest respect.

Israel, the prime minister explained, has set itself colossal goals. The attainment of each of these goals will bless mankind—will assist many nations beyond the narrow land which rolls from the Syrian border to the Gulf of Aqaba, from Dan to Eilat.

There is, first of all, the "ingathering of the exiles." Jews from seventy countries, of many colors, cultures, and historical experiences—from the sidewalks of New York to the tents of Iraq—are being welded into one people in Israel's "melting pot"—its "pressure cooker," the prime minister calls it.

Israel's experience in putting diverse people to a common schooling, in teaching them cleanliness in the Army, patriotism in the frontier settlement, and high aspirations at Hebrew University—this great exercise in building a unified nation and sloughing off centuries of contradictory customs is at the disposal of mankind.

"Harness the sun, sweeten the sea," the prime minister has said, setting research goals for Israel. When and if this country devises new techniques for utilizing solar radiation, or its Nuclear Physics Institute discovers a cheap method of distilling fresh water from sea water, this will be for the benefit of all dry countries.

"And the desert shall blossom as the rose." This lovely phrase states another practical goal of Israel. The prime minister went on:

"Our country is 60 per cent desert. Some of this was man-made; other areas have always been so. We have to remake it —we have to render the desert habitable.

"If we succeed, and there are signs that we shall succeed, we may help in the solution of a great world problem—causing to bloom vast desert areas of Asia and Africa, and thus raising living standards. Our desert settlements will show the way."

These are lofty objectives. Has Israel extended the helping hand to other nations?

While I was in Tel Aviv fifty delegates from cooperatives

in Asia and Africa—from Japan, Cambodia, India, Ceylon, French Sudan, Ghana, Nigeria, and Ethiopia—were attending a kind of "seminar for cooperatives" there, studying the Israeli techniques, visiting cooperatives around the land, exchanging experiences. Israeli officials pointed to this as exemplifying the prime minister's vision. (There is a land right next door to Israel which needs to make its desert bloom—the land of Egypt—but the Arab-Israeli feud prevents any cooperation whatsoever at present.)

Prime Minister Ben-Gurion gave his terms for a settlement with the Arab world—as well as his view of what prodigies Israel will have accomplished in another ten years. It recently celebrated its first ten years as a nation. But of that, more anon.

"What, to you, is the most encouraging development under way today in this new country?" I asked this self-made man, who at seventy-two declares that he is "still growing" and who is earnestly studying philosophy and science so that he may understand the paths his country must tread.

"What delights me most is the integration—I think you can call it that—of our immigrants," he replied.

"This is a great achievement, you know, bringing in these diverse people. In one month, people came from twenty-six different countries. These Jews had been separated in languages and cultures for thousands of years. Now the children all attend the same schools.

"We are gaining experience in raising the standards of people who, some of them, lived close to slavery; in other cases, the women were slaves, or the poor were slaves to the rich. We have raised their status, their self-respect, given women their natural rights, given men their normal abilities."

The Army, as well as the schools, has been a powerful factor here, the prime minister, who is obviously proud of the *élan* of his forces, declares.

"Our Army has iron discipline; it also has equality. The Army has taught young nomads cleanliness, city dwellers hard work. It inculcates comradeship, trust. The commander goes into battle first, in our forces.

"The labor federation has been an integrating instrument, too, with its cultural activities, its spirit of cooperation in building a new state.

"The world needs to learn coexistence, with its different standards, its differing races. We are showing that differences between peoples need not bar common achievement. All the world is now one country. Bring everyone up to the same level culturally and materially and you get at a root cause of war. We can help with our experience."

"What else encourages you here?" I asked Mr. Ben-Gurion.

"Our pioneering. We have a word for it—*chaluziuth*—it doesn't quite mean 'pioneering'; it means that a man should not be satisfied with merely believing a faith, but that he should live it. We had the idea of a 'return to Zion.' We did not merely preach it; we accomplished it.

"It will take many more decades to build our country. While history deprived us of many things and gave us a small poor country—one that is not 'flowing with milk and honey'—we cannot complain. We are intellectually as capable as other people. In our scientific achievements, in our university technology, we are not behind the biggest countries.

"Our young men are very promising."

So spoke, proudly, the Zionist who directed the Jewish Agency in Palestine before there was a Jewish state, who helped organize the Jewish Brigade in World War I, and who took over the prime ministership when, a few years back, the Israelis thought they were coming under increasingly militant pressures from the Arab states whose boundaries so narrowly circumscribe them. Today he divides his week between his prime minister's office in Jerusalem and his Defense Ministry in Tel Aviv. The government built him a fine new office in Tel Aviv, but he sticks frugally and loyally to old modest quarters.

Travel up and down this narrow-waisted state, as I have done, and you see what a decade of hard work, determination, and planning have accomplished in "face-lifting" and prodigious change.

In the less arid north, more forests are springing up. In greening wheat fields and new acreage, Israel is growing 70 per cent of its food, as contrasted with 40 per cent ten years ago. More factories are a-building. Liberal laws welcome foreign capital and foreign investors are interested in exploiting the Dead Sea minerals. Everywhere, highways are lined with eucalyptus trees and other fast-growing kinds—"Ben-Gurion's trees" they call them, for he urged this roadside planting.

In the midsouth, wide new vistas are being plowed by tractor, with hope for rain to supplement the water pipeline. Simple apartments are being hammered and cemented together to house latest immigrants in the new settlements, many located strategically close to the borders. Some settlements are inhabited largely by immigrants from Africa, some by Yemenite Jews, some by the influx from Europe.

At one point we drove through a swirling cloud of locusts —big metallic insects with strong wings—drifting in from Sinai. Lack of Israel-Arab cooperation prevents joint measures against this scourge, but Israeli planes were out spraying in a few hours. Further south, the real desert takes hold, on the way to the Gulf of Aqaba, yet archaeological research shows that this arid area held large towns and settlements centuries ago.

Israel is a land of contrasts, from cosmopolitan Tel Aviv on the Mediterranean to the rugged barrens and Grand Canyon-like landscape on the twisting road to the Dead Sea. Man's mastery of the land is by no means complete, but it is being skillfully tackled.

Israel has just celebrated its first ten years of accomplishment. What would the picture be ten years hence, I asked Prime Minister Ben-Gurion. He replied:

"As I look ahead, I see many more settlements in the Negev, throughout the arid south. I see the desert conquered and settled.

"I see Eilat, our port on the Gulf of Aqaba leading into the Red Sea, established as an international port, with flourishing trade relations between Israel and the peoples of Asia and Africa—as well as with the United States and Europe.

"I see the return of another million of our people, from Eastern Europe and the Middle East. We have already brought home one million Jews.

"And I would hope to see Israel enriched by the return of an elite group of Jews from the United States, Canada, the Argentine, England and South Africa, who would be pioneers in a special sense."

But a tremendous problem also loomed alongside those hopes. Would tomorrow's Israelis still gaze at hostile territory as they look out from Jerusalem to the mountains of Moab, and as they glance across the Dead Sea from their chemical plants on the western side? Would, in short, Israel be able to make its peace with the Arab world? I asked the prime minister what he felt would be the ultimate historical solution.

"There must first of all be more liberal and democratic regimes in the Arab countries. Regimes which can hardly control their own populace can hardly be expected to turn to making peace with Israel. The subject is too inflammable.

"When the Arab regimes have stabilized, their peoples will better understand what Israel can do to help improve their standards and welfare. This should help.

"Then these countries must be convinced that they cannot destroy Israel. Here the peoples of the free world can assist, by convincing the Arab countries that Israel is here to stay."

And what about the Arab refugees still in their miserable encampments? Would Israel definitely pay reparations?

"I believe that if the refugees knew the facts of the situation, they would be more willing to be resettled," the prime minister replied.

"There was a great change of heart among those in the Gaza Strip after the Sinai campaign. They had been told, 'Have patience, you will soon get back, you will even get Tel Aviv.' After the Sinai campaign, when the Arabs were badly defeated, these refugees refused to believe such promises any more and wanted to be resettled.

"As I have said before, peace can be agreed to in five minutes when the Arabs are ready. I will sit down and talk with President Nasser at any time, any minute.

"If Nasser would realize that peace is in his interest, we could get along. We had six thousand Egyptian prisoners of war after the Sinai campaign. We showed them our settlements, what we were doing in Palestine. They didn't want to fight us. Why should they?

"But you ask about the refugees. I will say this. If an agreement could be reached with the Arabs for resettling these refugees in the Arab countries—and if thereafter peace were really to prevail—we would make the biggest contribution to resettlement that we could. And we would be willing to contribute our experience as well as our money."

"And if there is no peace, and if the Arab states remain hostile?" I asked.

"We did stand at forty Arabs to one Israeli; now by our immigration program we have changed the ratio to twenty-two Arabs to one Jew. Still this is quite a disproportion. The Arab air forces are four times as big as ours. I think that all of this entitles us to help from the free nations which have no interest in our destruction.

"We have a messianic belief that we must accomplish the redemption of our own people. So we seek the return of as many Jews to our land as wish to come—where they will be free to live according to their desires and ideas, and to create a society fulfilling the vision of our prophets.

"We want to build a society where there is no oppression, no exploitation, where there is mutual help and where the ideal will be followed that 'you shall love your fellow man as yourself.' "

The Israelis are, indeed, finding that their experience, their technical know-how, their institutions of learning, can be helpful to other lands. They cannot reach across to the Arabs, and so they are reaching around them to promote cordial relations with Ghana and other emerging African countries, with Burma and other new lands of Asia. At Hebrew University, of the fifty-two hundred students, seventy are from various countries of Asia and Africa.

But a sharp question remained. Does Israel really know the Arab world today? Is the latter progressing, modernizing, more than Israel realizes?

"In ten years I have had no direct contact with the Arabs," Prime Minister Ben-Gurion replied. "Before that, I had contact with simple Arabs as I worked in the fields. I met others in the Turkish University. And as chairman of the Jewish Agency I dealt with many. I don't know what their thinking is now."

Here, to an outsider, is a situation which could carry great danger to the Israel of the future, ten years hence. The Arabs, many of them, are no longer as backward as when the Zionists lost direct contact with them. The time could conceivably come when the Arab states would even gain sufficient military ability to defeat Israel by force of arms.

But whether or no, will not many Israelis one day have to raise their concept of the Arabs, and begin to see them as equals? Are not these Arabs to be numbered among the "fellow men" that are to be loved? To carry forward sufficiently with its great vision of assisting humanity, out of the riches of its own pioneering experience, will not Israel have to make more diligent efforts to arrive at an understanding with its Arab neighbors?

A very courageous people, drawn from the four corners of the earth, are planting forests where goats grazed in past centuries, are piping water to desert settlements, locating kibbutzim on the imperiled boundaries, discovering ancient reservoirs in the Negev, enlarging citrus orchards, building the port at Eilat, mining copper, manufacturing their own generators, probing nuclear energy.

The long history of spoliation in Palestine is being dramatically reversed. The "ingathering of the exiles" continues. But doughty Mr. Ben-Gurion and his people have still to find some way of applying their idealism to their Arab neighbors if Israel is to cease being a beleaguered land.

12

U Nu

(BURMA)

Rangoon

"IN THIS very room I urged upon Soviet Marshal Zhukov that he should visit the United States." In these words, U Nu, Burma's most widely known and respected leader, epitomized the role which he and his country have sought to play in this difficult and challenging postwar period. Nor has this role been easy for either.

"Zhukov agreed that a visit to Washington would be a very desirable thing. 'But,' he asked, 'how would I get an invitation?' " U Nu continued.

Georgi K. Zhukov never went to Washington—Secretary of State Dulles withdrew President Eisenhower's tentative invitation—and we know what happened to Marshal Zhukov. He was eventually dismissed from office by Soviet Premier Nikita S. Khrushchev.

But U Nu had emphasized his discussion with Marshal Zhukov in Rangoon to illustrate his own preferred role in world affairs.

This is to go about in his diplomatic contacts telling nations good things about one another.

"I tell the Russians the good things that I know about America—that you are not seeking world domination, that you want peace. And," he added with a sly smile, "I tell your people the good things that I know about the Russians."

Unworldly, this? Ineffectual? U Nu, who may one day be re-elected prime minister, had just emerged from a week of wearing "the robe"—a week of Buddhist contemplation. He appeared as fresh in thought, as serene, on this sunny morning of our interview, as the clear air of Burma's mild winter.

This happy impression was perhaps enhanced by U Nu's round, smiling face surmounted by the gay *gaung baung*, a close-fitting headdress with flowing bow, and by the informal-appearing long-sleeved, high-necked jacket (*ingyi*) and the long saronglike skirt he wore (the *longyi*). These seemed like holiday robes rather than the attire of a politician who had given Burma honest, if not always efficient, government since independence in January, 1948.

Burma is a small agricultural country the size of Texas, with 19 to 20 million people. It doesn't carry great physical weight in world affairs. But it urges conciliation where it can. And so it was that U Nu had suggested that Marshal Zhukov visit the United States and see the American people for himself. He was of course talking to the wrong man; his project was under veto from either the Kremlin or Washington, perhaps both.

But this did not deter this prominent Buddhist, whose unclouded, smiling countenance suggests that, through daily contemplation, he has attained a large measure of inner serenity.

There is, however, a matter of great practicality, much closer to home, which must be tackled before U Nu or anyone else will be able to restore parliamentary democracy to Burma.

And that is the drift toward corruption and strong-arm tactics which has beset Burmese politics and political parties and which has brought into power, as at least a temporary antidote, the "caretaker government" of General Ne Win.

General Ne Win and U Nu are Burma's twin spokesmen today. Ne Win steadily refuses to see visiting journalists.

The general is a hard-working soldier, who has little taste for the complexities of politics. He is vigorously opposed to the Communists, whose insurgent armies he has had to battle continuously upcountry as Burma's chief of staff. And he would like to see his country's stalled postwar reconstruction acquire a new lease of enthusiasm.

U Nu had been Burma's respected national leader through ten perplexing, touch-and-go years. He is a man whose impeccable honesty and religious sense recommended him when a senseless assassination in 1947 wiped out virtually the entire wartime resistance leadership of the fledgling state. But he has been a prime minister who did not quite come to grips with the ruthlessness which can beset an untutored nation's politics.

When the Anti-Fascist People's Freedom League—a large mouthful but the governing party of Burma for ten years—split, U Nu, to retain a majority, allied himself with left-wing parties. The right-wing of the AFPFL acquired arms, and it became increasingly clear that elections scheduled to be held in the fall would be violent. The country faced total disruption of government.

In this crisis a group of officers served on Prime Minister U Nu a demand for changes. The outcome was a proposal by U Nu himself that General Ne Win—who had once before, in 1949, been persuaded to enter the government as defense minister to fight the Communist insurgency—should this time take over as prime minister for a period of six months. The general agreed and was duly confirmed by a comfortable majority in the Parliament. The six-months' period was later extended to the end of 1959.

General Ne Win has done a superb job of "cleanup," in several senses of the word. Soldiers swept the filthy streets and unplugged the clogged drains of Rangoon, once known (in prewar British days) as "the cleanest city in Asia." Hoarders, profiteers, venal politicians—and motorists who had let their driver's licenses expire—were arrested right and left. Almost everyone has applauded Ne Win's new broom. If General Ne Win continues to win favor by his forthright actions, and if he should be able to make major headway in extinguishing the insurgency upcountry—where several Communist and guerrilla armies have been battling the government since the dawn of independence—there might well be a popular clamor for him to remain in office. This could be arranged constitutionally if he ran for election himself, in some "sure" district.

The civil war upcountry does seem to be collapsing. Simultaneously, the split which has wrecked Burma's governing party still persists. And now a group of politically minded younger officers have sided with the anti-U Nu faction, known as the "Stable" AFPFL. Will Burma indeed resort permanently to a military solution, as has happened in Thailand, Pakistan, and other neighboring countries?

What does U Nu say about all this?

"Burma's most encouraging manifestation since the beginnings of our independence has been the determination of the people to perpetuate their freedom," says the former prime minister.

"This government by Prime Minister Ne Win, which I myself proposed, is only a temporary phase. I heartily approve of his cleanup program, his vigorous measures. But in the long run we shall have to act through elections and elected officials.

"A democratic regime has its tribulations, you know. Take the squatters who have come to live in Rangoon. If you forcibly oust them, you lose a vast number of votes, and votes are necessary to win office. So instead of using force, you have to find suitable alternative housing, you have to get transport, you have to institute rehabilitation measures. It is all very costly, and slow business. For those who don't need to catch votes, it's much easier."

Turning again to the topic of world affairs, I asked U Nu what further international role Burma could play, assuming that the domestic crisis was eased and a stable course recharted.

"Buddhism inculcates peace," he replied. "Thus we in Burma naturally have an obligation to accept the gospel of peace, to work for peace. One of the five precepts that every Buddhist must accept is to abstain from killing. This should govern, very basically, our foreign policy.

"We have good relations with most of our neighbors. There is unfortunately very little economic cooperation among the Bandung powers due to politics." (The Bandung powers are the twenty-nine Asian and African countries which met at Bandung, Indonesia, in 1955.)

I questioned U Nu concerning the state of relations with his biggest neighbor, Communist China, with whom Burma shares a mountainous, thousand-mile border.

"Our own people," he said, "simply refuse to accept communism. Buddhism and communism do not mix. Some areas upcountry tolerate Communist bands—because they have to; the bands have arms. But as soon as the village people are assured that the government is locating forces near-by and that these will not be withdrawn, they turn on the bandits. And they reveal their hidden arms caches."

U Nu preferred not to talk about his own special method of dealing with Peking, which refuses to settle certain boundary disputes and seeks to strengthen its hold over Chinese residents through the lending activities of its two banks in Rangoon.

From other knowledgeable quarters, however, it was disclosed that the patent "Burma formula" is gently to remind Peking of those clauses in the Bandung charter against aggressions and encroachments which it is currently violating. Sometimes this is effective; sometimes it is not. Obviously Burma treads with considerable care, seeking not to offend Peking too much. The Burmese press has had surprisingly little to say about Peking's behavior in Tibet.

"You know that we are a very young nation," U Nu resumed. "In 1948, three months after independence, a tremendous rebellion broke out; it would have been enough to finish off most governments. But Burma is still carrying on. We need time to set our house in order."

Burma's future would seem to lie in the triple concerns of U Nu, General Ne Win, and the young Army officers. It is the only country where the gross national product has not reached prewar percentages. In some areas it suffered wartime destruction equal to that of Germany. Today the United States is aiding Burma with loans and equipment—police equipment for moving against the insurgents, trucks and bulldozers for shoring up the dikes and restoring the rice paddies. Relations between Burma and Washington are good.

"Your State Department is doing better with its foreign

policy," said U Nu with a frankness and unself-consciousness which has startled many a hearer. "You are appreciating the value of sturdy neutrality in a nation." In past years he has advised American listeners to be less "obsessed" by fear of communism, has told them that "you are a great and strong nation; don't let yourselves be upset by little things."

As a kind of theological uncle, he feels that the countries of Asia should strive to join their "spiritual" outlook to the "materialistic" progress of the West. He frequently speaks in abstract ideals, save when he is on the campaign platform, when he can be a canny and persuasive politician.

U Nu is a most articulate spokesman for Burma. He stands head and shoulders above most Burmese politicians. But the immensely difficult problem of "making democracy work" in a land only recently independent (1949) has beset Burma as it has beset other Asian lands. While the "Stable" faction of the Anti-Fascist People's Freedom League under U Ba Swe and the "Clean" faction of the AFPFL under U Nu have traded charges of graft, nepotism, and the employment of strong-arm tactics, the Communist-front minority party, known as the National United Front, has been gleefully profiting by the confusion.

The military men who have sided with the "Stable" group contend that they are acting only to thwart the Communists and their Communist-front party (the Communist party itself is banned in Burma). Meantime, U Nu represents the one individual pledged to democratic government who could probably win at the polls, *if* a genuinely free and unrigged election could be held.

General Ne Win has pledged free elections, but at this writing the business of cleaning up Burma still engages his attention. Politicians of both wings of the AFPFL and the National United Front are languishing in jail. The average Burman seems fairly content to let Ne Win continue to wield his broom, if he will. U Nu believes, however, that if he and his followers are permitted by the Army to wage an unintimidated, unfettered election campaign, they can restore genuinely democratic rule to Burma.

Burma's choice, in the long run, would seem to lie between paternalistic efficiency and a rather shaky democracy.

13

Sukarno

(INDONESIA)

Jakarta

A CONVOY of motorcycles, sirens whining, circled the Kemajoran Airport drive, followed by four jeeploads of soldiers, then a shiny black sedan. At the "VIP Lounge" the automobile halted, and a jaunty figure stepped out, a rather handsome man, sunglasses over eyes, black Indonesian cap on his head, carrying a tiny silver-and-black cane like a swagger stick.

This was Sukarno, president of an archipelago of islands which, measured against North America on a map, would extend from San Francisco to Bermuda.

President, yes, of a people close to 100 million strong who, with their proud determination, could become the fourth most powerful force in Asia—after Japan, China, and India. Here was a man with an engineering degree but the outlook and sensitivity of a poet and revolutionary.

The president stepped briskly into the lounge, where waited a few members of his new National Council (for "guided democracy"), some military officers and foreign attachés come to bid him Godspeed, a covey of women secretaries in colorful blouses and batik skirts, and his wife and young son.

He beamingly saluted the six-year-old boy, who gravely saluted back, to the delight of all. Then he kissed his wife and sat down with her.

The crowds which would hang on his words, laugh at his sallies, draw meaning to their lives and unity to their purpose from his speeches, were absent today. For this was to be a rest trip to Bali.

But there was a charm of personality about the man even as he chatted amiably with friends. To paraphrase Edwin Arlington Robinson, he "glittered when he talked."

With a flick of the swagger stick he granted permission to Gordon Converse to take his picture. I approached and, after introduction by a young lady from the Foreign Office who had studied at the University of Michigan, asked him what current development in Indonesia made him proudest.

"Education," he quietly answered. "We are exceedingly proud of our educational strides. We have ten times more students in schools than when the Dutch left."

Any authority on Indonesia, any United States Embassy official, would heartily agree with the president. A national literacy which was 7 per cent in 1954 is now estimated variously as having risen to 40 or 50 per cent. There is an unslakable thirst for learning. Schools are frequently on three shifts a day. Where there was but one university, now nine provinces have universities—some with exceedingly bare library shelves, but carrying on nevertheless.

The American Embassy has a voluminous correspondence with young Indonesians wishing to study and to travel in the United States. It does what it can with its International Exchange Program and International Cooperation Administration provisions, and the Ford Foundation is at work here, too.

Indonesia wants to learn—fast. He who provides books, training, newspapers, skills, teachers, will do much to sway Indonesia's future. Moscow and Peking are aware of this; so is Washington! The United States is doing a good job here, offering know-how, training, ideas, and experience with "no strings attached."

"What is Indonesia's central role in the world society today?" I asked the president.

"Our desire is to work steadily for peace," he replied. "We have, at home, the tremendous task of building a nation. We cannnot afford blocs. We cannot contemplate war."

Peace is the preoccupation of many Asian nations, Burma, Malaya, India among them. They have so much to do at home that alliances, extra military expenditures, are totally unpalatable.

But Indonesia goes at this business of nation-building with a special vehemence, almost chip on shoulder. Indonesians are out to show the world that they are not "little brown brothers," to be treated like children. They can, and will, manage their own affairs, thank you. No patronizer need apply, even though bearing a foreign-aid program.

President Sukarno did not need to say this. All of his speeches glow with Indonesian pride—and have done so since preindependence days. For his early demands and agitation for freedom he spent long months in jail.

"Indonesia is ob-vi-ous," the president emphasized in excellent English. "It is not a little nation off in a corner somewhere. It is centrally located—geographically, politically, economically."

Indeed, yes. Geographically Indonesia's myriad islands, big and small, constitute the crucial bridge linking the Philippines, Singapore, Malaya, and Australia.

Politically, as one of the five cosponsors of the Bandung Conference, it is a leader in Asian-African solidarity. A half dozen Asian-African societies have offices in Jakarta. There is a women's league, a parliamentary association, a youth organization. As a Bandung power, Indonesia is almost fanatically neutralist.

Economically, Indonesia is rich in oil, rubber, tin, copra, coffee, tea, and spices (remember the Spice Islands?). It has the ingredients of potent nationhood.

Shortly an officer on the airfield barked a command. The president's plane was ready—usually a Soviet transport, gift of the Soviet Union. But today that plane was being overhauled, and he used a military aircraft. The president kissed his family, saluted, and walked out on the runway.

This is the chief executive who has been essaying somewhat the role in Indonesia that Jawaharlal Nehru fills in India: unifier of many areas and customs, spokesman for freedom (Merdeka!), igniter of enthusiasms for building a modern nation.

A few weeks earlier he had made a fast tour of the Moluccas and the eastern areas of Indonesia, as exhaustive a trip as any presidential primary performance by Estes Kefauver. Newsmen and ambassadors who trailed along testify to the pace. The president would make two- and three-hour speeches each day. Then in the evening he would join in a native dancing party—something alarmingly akin to square dancing and just about as restful. Then he would be up at dawn for the trip to the next island.

This was outlying territory, and the question was whether the president would be as popular there as he is in Java, the central island. But the same magnetism worked with the outlanders. They laughed and cheered, were grateful for attention, and never found his speeches tedious.

This is what President Sukarno does best. He has been called a rabble-rouser, only happy when he is out haranguing a crowd, skilled only in speechmaking. A kindlier appraisal, by some who believe they know the president well, is that he likes, even loves, the people, derives inspiration from them, basks in their approval. There is rapport between personality and populace. Whatever the right analysis, his is a mentality suited to the main job at hand.

He is not a good administrator, does not care for desk work. This is why Indonesia has not had competent administration in the government until recently; why the Army, under its chief of staff, Major General Abdul Haris Nasution, has sought to insert a little ramrod discipline into the regime to get necessary things done which had long been postponed by party haggling and political conniving.

Popularity has its hazards for democracy, of course. Recently President Sukarno made a moving speech in which he alluded to his preferred epitaph. He said something like this:

"Don't write down 'Dr. Sukarno, president, engineer, world statesman, and so on.' Just write 'Sukarno, who spoke what was in the people's hearts.' "

The question which must always be asked, however, is whether the political leader is enunciating the wishes and aims of the people or whether he is injecting his own views, his own ideas and philosophy, into their consciousness. In a brand-new nation perhaps there has to be a little of both.

It was shortly after President Sukarno's visit to Moscow and Peking that he announced that since Indonesian democracy was not working well—too many parties, too much corruption—he was going over to a new concept, "guided democracy." The Cabinet and Parliament were to be "advised" hereafter by a council composed of functional groups: trade unions, religious leaders, youth movements, intelligentsia, women's organizations, the press, artists, businessmen.

Though this setup helped to see Indonesia through the worst phases of the revolt of groups in the outlying islands which were demanding more autonomy and less corruption from Jakarta, and though the Indonesian economy is slightly on the upswing after touching rock bottom, President Sukarno has never quite been able to define "guided democracy."

Much has been written in alarm about it. It is probably true that the president was impressed by what he saw at Peking (before the days of the communes) and by Madame Sun Yat-sen's explanation, delivered at Jakarta during a visit. She maintained that Communist China believed in both "freedom of expression" and "freedom from want," but that because it must concentrate on the latter it would have to shelve, temporarily, the former.

However, a high Indonesian foreign ministry official has said: "We won't give up the secret ballot or representation in Parliament. But we cannot assume, in an undeveloped country, that democracy will work as well as it does in Britain or the United States. We need some kind of extra 'X' ingredient here."

This official did not define the extra "X" ingredient. Regimes in Pakistan, the Sudan, even Burma, would like to know what this "X" may be. The nearest President Sukarno himself has come to a definition is to say it means "effective leadership." This could mean the president himself or the Army's new intervention at key points in the economy and administration.

The Army under able General Nasution has quietly inserted effective Army-trained officials into key positions in the government and is acting to clear up legislative tangles and other governmental weaknesses which the feuding political parties have not been able to solve in all the exciting years since the proclamation of independence in 1954.

Perhaps this is not quite "guided democracy," but many foreign observers in Jakarta feel that, as of now and in these inexperienced days, it is a tremendously salutary development.

It would be easy here to exclaim, "Ah, the Army is about to take over totally the government as has happened in Pakistan, the Sudan, and Thailand." But this conclusion would overlook the special character of this Army which so recently fought a war of independence and is closely and sympathetically identified with the people of Indonesia. And it would be overlooking the caliber of General Nasution, he of the cool head, the tact, and the ardor for the "middle way." It would overlook the fact that President Sukarno remains the popular head of state.

Even benevolent Army intrusion into the government is not recommended democratic practice, but in a government weak in administration and in the economic realm the Indonesian Army is becoming a significant stabilizing factor.

For example, Indonesia had been without a mining law ever since independence. This meant that the big oil companies actually had operated here on mere verbal approval from the government. Now the Army has placed Colonel Prengadi in the Cabinet as deputy to the minister of industries. His initial comment was, "Now we will have a mining law. It may not be perfect, but it will be there."

Most important of all from the Western point of view is the fact that the Army's influence has been distinctly and steadily anti-Communist. And the Army has been friendly to the United States. By the end of the fiscal year, 320 officers, including the two deputy chiefs of staff, had been trained in the United States. In the darkest days of the rebellion it may have been the influence of American-trained officers on General Nasution which kept suspicion against Americans from boiling over.

When General Nasution reassumed the post of chief of staff in 1955, he spent the first two years getting Communist influence out of the Army. Now he is working beyond the Army. It was the Army on which the government could safely call to oust Communist-led labor contingents from Dutch properties which they had occupied at the end of 1957. When Communist-led unions ordered strikes at seaports, General Nasution stepped in and said: "No strikes." There weren't any.

Potent has been Army influence in postponing the national elections scheduled for September, 1959. With the Communists evidencing vast strength in local election campaigns and with other parties squabbling, it was apparent that the Communists would capture the government in any national election. Now the election has been postponed to 1960, and there may be further postponements. Army spokesmen insist this is only to give time for the other non-Communist parties to reorganize themselves effectively.

How does President Sukarno feel about all this? one might well ask. The answer given in Jakarta is that he is not opposing General Nasution. Dr. Sukarno still has vast popularity with the Indonesian people. He may be glad to have a firmer hand on administration. In this dual setup, Dr. Sukarno supplies the popular appeal while the Army supplies the needed stability.

Those who are still doubtful may gain some assurance from General Nasution's own statement in mid-November of 1958, when he declared at the Megelang Military Academy: "We are in no way going to copy the situations that prevailed in some Latin-American countries where the military became a political tool, neither those in Western Europe where the Army is a dead instrument. . . . We take the middle way."

Certainly the army is not junta-minded. General Nasution favors the United States and American training for his officers because, he says frankly, he can get United States equipment readily; the United States is close at hand in SEATO and the Seventh Fleet patrols the Pacific.

He is also aware, as some Indonesians are not, that American strength in the Western Pacific serves to protect Indonesia from any possible aggression.

Meanwhile President Sukarno remains an undisguised, unrepentant neutralist. On his latest world tour, slated to take him to Moscow and to the United States, he was still tub-thumping against colonialism. When he visited Ankara, the Turks tried to persuade him that colonialism was a fading shibboleth, but he still feels—strongly—that the Dutch should get out of their slice of New Guinea (West Irian).

Some Americans have been miffed because, after Sukarno visited the United States a few years ago and said he liked Americans, he went off to Moscow and Peking and thereafter said nice things about the Communists, too. This, to the president, was simply and frankly playing the role of neutral.

Those who know him well affirm that the president, himself an extrovert and a lively fellow, likes America and Americans. Simultaneously the Soviet success in lifting a nation from serfdom to major stature in forty years is impressive to him. President Sukarno and his government are not taking sides. But of late they seem convinced that United States' foreign-aid programs are not designed to force or lure Indonesia into a Western alliance.

The suspicion of American intentions, which boiled over when a rebel flier who happened to be an American was captured, has evaporated. United States Ambassador Howard Jones, a kindly, thoughtful, understanding career service diplomat, has done an excellent job in Jakarta.

President Sukarno thought he saw American "imperialism" at work when the United States Marines landed in Lebanon. When they did not push on to Iraq and when they eventually withdrew, to the president and many highly placed Indonesians this was indication that the Communist allegations about "Yankee imperialism" were false.

Not so long ago, President Sukarno, like John L. Lewis in his CIO days and President Beneš in Czechoslovakia, thought he could "use" the Communists—welcome them into his government—to further his own policies. More recently not only the Soviet behavior in Hungary but the Communists' own arrogant behavior locally have made a major impression on government circles here. The leftward drift in Indonesia seems, at least for the present, to be halted.

In his preindependence speeches President Sukarno frequently referred to freedom, political independence, as a "golden bridge." In a 1933 booklet he wrote, "On the far side of that bridge we will rebuild our society."

Now Indonesia is on the far side of that bridge. The road is pretty rough. Foreign exchange has dribbled away. The birth rate is appallingly high. Rebels still plot in outlying islands. Foreign investment is skittish about coming to Indonesia.

Yet at the same time Indonesia has tremendous assets. These people intend to make a name for themselves. Women are remarkably emancipated for a Moslem—for any Asian—country. One woman runs one of Indonesia's top newspapers; another is chairman of Parliament's Foreign Relations Committee; another heads the prime minister's secretariat. As one former freedom fighter explained it to me, "We do not want a theocratic state. We are Moslems, yes, but we are also Indonesians."

America—the West—can help this country over the rough spots with grants and credits, with scholarships and travelships, with ideas and philosophy. President Sukarno read avidly during his lonely months in prison from many cultures and philosophies. He can quote readily from Lincoln and Jefferson—and from Marx and Sun Yat-sen. These people are eager to soak up the best the world has to offer. I believe they have the intelligence to discern between the principled and the spurious.

In this picture President Sukarno is a catalyst, a transmitter of ideas, a symbol for his countrymen. He is also a shrewd political infighter who knows how to play one opponent off against another.

Indonesia is quite likely to make its way in the world. With a unifier and an enunciator of Indonesian hopes and dreams like President Sukarno leading the way, the road uphill may not seem so steep.

14

Garcia

(PHILIPPINES)

Manila

THE PHILIPPINE Republic today is a nation in search of its destiny. There are ideas aplenty concerning "international roles" in this lovely archipelago—brilliant ideas—but execution is ofttimes faulty.

The Philippines, it has been suggested, should serve as a showcase of Asian democracy, a demonstration of the excellent send-off which the United States gives to its former colony.

But the showcase is in disrepair: graft and corruption need to be rooted out. The will to reform needs to be stronger.

Another suggestion, this from President Garcia, is that the republic, because it is an amalgam of Asian and Western cultures, can serve signally as a "prism" through which Asia and the West "can view each other with greater clarity and understanding."

This is a noble idea, and these friendly people, with their able diplomatic representation across free Asia, can do and have done much to promote a better understanding among suspicious new Asian regimes of Washington's purposes and the West's motivations.

But perhaps the boldest idea of all is another spoken by President Garcia from his private office in Malacanan Palace: that the free nations of Asia "explore forms of joint action to offset the economic-warfare pressures" of Communist China and the Communist bloc and that Manila lead this joint effort.

In other words, the free Asian countries which have a common denominator of interest anyway in their respective economic development programs, and a common plight in that each has felt economic pressure from Peking, should get together and devise joint means of resisting that pressure.

In an address to the Manila Overseas Press Club, President Garcia declared, expanding on his proposal: "Among the members of the free Asian community there must develop a broad and sympathetic understanding of each other's thinking, problems and national objectives. With such understanding we can explore the common ground upon which a common economic, political, and spiritual defense may be based and collective action undertaken. . . .

"Red military aggressions in Asia largely ceased when SEATO was born. Now the weapons have changed. How are we to respond to this new challenge? Collective purpose, collective action, and a pooling of resources were effective in the military phase; why not in the current situation?"

There are experts who suggest that the Philippine Republic's action in seeking stronger ties with Asia means weaker ties with the United States. Undeniably Philippine-American relations are in a period of coolness and estrangement.

It is true that American economic aid and currency-stabilization allocations to the Philippines have not been what President Garcia and his officials would like. It is also true that Washington has held down on its financial help to Manila because it is felt that too much of the assistance was being dissipated in graft and corruption—that rich officials were getting richer and the poor were getting only unemployment.

The aid tangle needs to be straightened out. So does the squabble over the American military bases in the islands. It will be extra difficult if Philippine politicos have concluded that their only hope of winning elections lies in a campaign of "anti-Americanism."

It is true that Washington has often "taken Filipino friendship for granted." One of the most difficult financial maneuvers in the world is to extend foreign aid with just enough "controls attached" so that the recipient country uses the aid wisely, yet is not affronted.

But fortunately, despite temporary estrangements, ideas can be shared and can lead to a reduction of disagreement. President Garcia supplied many ideas in his written responses.

The president was campaigning at Cebu City when I reached Manila. It was impossible to see him and maintain my schedule. So he kindly agreed to write down his answers. The following are his responses to the many questions I put to him:

Q.: Each country, Mr. President, has some essential role to play in today's history. What in your opinion is the special role or destiny of the Republic of the Philippines?

A.: The human race today is afflicted and threatened by two major divisions. The first, between individual human freedom and the enslavement of Communist statism, is the gravest and is irreconcilable as long as communism clings to its aggressive goal of world subjugation. The second division, which keeps free Asians from complete cooperation with the free West in pursuit of mutually beneficial objectives, stems from the colonial experience.

How quickly this rift is bridged may well decide the outcome of the more serious division. In one respect, our experience as Asians is unique. Our final battle for freedom was fought, not with gun and sword, but with ideas and ideals. Thus, our relations today with the former sovereign power, America, are not embittered by memories of violence. In matters of common interest and concern we cooperate as friendly equals in an atmosphere of mutual trust and respect.

We furthermore see the possibility of serving—by virtue of our unique experience—as a sort of prism through which Asia and the West can view each other with greater clarity and understanding. With a culture representing an amalgam of the Malayan, Latin- and Anglo-American cultural elements we can, and are willing, to be a bridge between Asia and the free West.

Q.: What further needs to be done to enable the Philippines to realize its full destiny?

A.: Problems of transition and forced growth beset us as they do every other nation seeking to overcome the technological lag between Asian societies and the West. Left to our own resources exclusively the rate of progress necessarily will be slow. The process could be speeded if each member of the world community concerned recognized the need for common and collective effort and took appropriate action. Trade, investment, and a pooling of experience are typical areas inviting action.

Q.: What in your view, sir, is the most encouraging or constructive development presently under way in the Philippines?

A.: In terms of what we see as our role in world affairs, we can view with great satisfaction the steadily increasing flow of visits from our Asian neighbors, seriously purposeful visits. Some come to study our approach to social and political problems, others for more specific technical training. Filipino technicians and professionals are increasingly in demand for service in neighboring countries. Reports we have of our neighbors' reactions to these personal contacts are most gratifying, and their sincerity is borne out by the fact that the traffic is increasing.

Q.: What would you list among the most harmful or unconstructive activities in your country today, and how can these be eradicated?

A.: Communist subversion and infiltration continues to be a heavy burden and a costly one. This phase of the Communist's unceasing warfare against free peoples is more difficult to cope with than outright military aggression, because the enemy takes cover behind legitimate democratic institutions, making unwitting tools of those he intends to destroy or enslave.

Of less but still serious concern are the excesses of partisan politics. While understandable in a young democracy savoring the hard-won satisfactions of self-government, our zest for political contest threatens to become a vice. High-pitched propaganda battles, designed more for impact than accurate information, begin too long before and last too long after our elections.

The result is an almost constant level of excitement which distracts us from the urgent business of nation-building and planning, and blurs the picture of our actual national situation and condition. My feeling is that both these ills can be relieved by one remedy: the democratic society must become a working organization in all its benign aspects, giving the satisfactions free men expect of it, and affording the constructive creative outlets man requires for growth.

Q.: The late President Magsaysay had begun to instill a new spirit of loyalty and sacrifice in this country. How can this spirit be continued and intensified so as to root out graft and corruption?

A.: The problem of graft and corruption is inseparable from the economic problem. Evildoers grow bolder as the stakes grow larger. Until economic controls, with their high premium on evasion, can be relaxed safely, our law enforcement agencies are exerting every effort to expose and punish the guilty.

Q.: The nations of free Asia, around the periphery of Communist China, are alerting themselves to Peking's attempts at intimidation and economic penetration. Should these countries, including the Philippines, band together to present a united front against the Communist threat?

A.: When speaking at the Manila Overseas Press Club, I advanced the proposal that the free nations of Asia, having a common denominator of interest in their respective economic development programs, explore forms of joint action to offset Red bloc economic warfare pressures. In selecting or devising an agency for this purpose, due consideration would have to be given to the diverse defense and political policies of the participants.

Q.: Can Japan's apparent interest in promoting capital development programs in the smaller nations of Asia be helpful?

A.: Japan's advanced technology could help speed Asia's economic development provided Japan's approach recognizes its partners as sovereign equals, and not as satellite raw materials sources for its industrial complex. I have reason to believe, after visiting Japan and talking with its leaders, that the Japanese are sincere in seeking healthy economic relationships with their neighbors.

Q.: What about economic aid from the United States?

A.: The less strings attached thereto, the more genuine such assistance will appear to be. The donor will gain in genuine esteem and gratitude and the donee will acquire a deeper sense of responsibility in using wisely the aids. Too much interference in the use of the given aid and too little confidence in the sense of responsibility of a donee is not conducive to good public relations at the international level.

It is obvious that President Garcia has important things to say. And it is also obvious that Manila has a list of grievances against Washington, most of them concerning aid funds or military bases.

President Garcia's interview recorded here suggests the spirit in which problems might be tackled. A calculated program of anti-Americanism would hardly be as effective.

I suppose the basic problem confronting the Philippines is epitomized in the courtyard scene I spotted while taxiing about Manila. Banana fronds were growing luxuriantly in this ruined garden; the lovely residence had been destroyed by the Japanese in World War II and never rebuilt.

The Filipinos are never likely to find themselves starving. Nature is too bountiful in the rice paddies, the coconut groves, the pineapple plantations, and the vegetable patches beside the barrios. But the Filipinos presently are exhibiting neither the colossal energy of the Japanese, the intense "We'll do it ourselves or bust" of the Indonesians, nor the sophisticated efficiency of the new Malayan Federation.

The Republic of the Philippines needs to expand its industrial base, but five-year plans are not being followed resolutely. Charges and disclosures of graft and corruption are causing deep splits in the ranks of the governing Nationalista party. As a nation early attaining its freedom from colonial status and possessed of a splendidly heroic war record, the Philippines is not, in many major ways, living up to expectations.

Searching for causes, some observers cite Toynbee's theory of "response to challenge." The Filipinos have it relatively easy. Up in chilly, crowded Japan the populace knows it must struggle to survive. Not so in the warm, lush Philippines.

Yet this reasoning overlooks what the late President Ramón Magsaysay was achieving before his tragic passing. He was stirring to life a Philippine identity, he was promoting honesty, he was building hope. A "strong man," he was transforming the old loyalty from family to country by his personal appeal and example. He was available to all who had problems. The public felt he was getting things done that needed to be done.

A new nation needs a strong executive; this is the experience all over Asia. It is complained that President Garcia is lacking in this essential. When there is a weak executive, the untutored political parties spend their days squabbling. Tax documents disappear from the revenue offices. Precious foreign exchange dollars are siphoned away by venal officials and businessmen.

There has been some crackdown on corruption and the

picture is not all black. The International Cooperation Administration declares itself pleased with the way the Philippines has tackled some of its programs. Production indexes for mining, manufacturing, and agriculture have shown a slow rise.

Obviously the United States would like to see its protégé, the Filipino, take a prominent place in the Asian procession of progress. So far Washington has lent or given the Philippines more than a billion dollars in aid since the war's end. Perhaps President Garcia can still wield his power more effectively. But until the house cleaning takes place, Washington hesitates to boost its allocations.

The banana stalks were almost ripe for picking in that bombed-out courtyard when I left Manila. The friendly, easy-going, anti-Communist Philippines will survive. But one of these days the beautiful residence will need to be strongly rebuilt. The task seems to await a government mustering courage, conviction, and no corruption.

15

Abdul Rahman

(MALAYA)

Kuala Lumpur

THE FIRST prime minister of Malaya, Tengku Abdul Rahman, has recently adopted two children. One is a little Chinese girl, Meriam, aged five, who came from a leper settlement. The other is a little Malay boy, Sulieman, aged four, who came from an orphanage.

In the middle of our interview, the tengku (we should translate it, "the prince," for he is of royal lineage) interrupted himself, as Meriam walked by, to say, "The little girl is very lovable."

No action I know of by this moderate, balanced, farsighted, avuncular man who heads the new Federation of Malaya better illustrates his character, or suggests the task to which he has dedicated his country than his adoption of two youngsters of different races.

For, in a succinct word, Tengku Abdul Rahman is seeking to build a biracial state—of Malay and Chinese—which shall develop a country of vastly rich potential in harmony, finding common cause in a brilliant future.

And when one realizes what this example should mean to

India and Pakistan—where the old communal feeling still seethes between Hindu and Moslem—and to France and Algeria, and to all the other racial plagued areas of the earth, one realizes the worth of the mission to which the Tengku has dedicated himself.

Malaya is 49 per cent Malay, 38 per cent Chinese, 12 per cent Indian. Can it become an effective triracial or biracial state, as in English-French Canada, another member of the same Commonwealth?

"Once upon a time here, the British pursued a policy of divide and rule," the prime minister observes. "Many Europeans laughed when I called for an independent biracial state. Some said, 'On Merdeka Day there will be robbing and killing—see what happened in India and Pakistan!' But I said, 'Wait and see.' "

Nothing did happen. The federation was safely launched August 31, 1957, amid general rejoicing. So far, so good.

But the task lies ahead. Many Chinese want their language to be one of the official languages, alongside Malay. Others worry that Malayan special privileges will be enacted. Still other young Chinese feel an affinity for Peking. Malays, on the other hand, worry that Singapore's Chinese majority may be added to Malaya, giving the Chinese a majority throughout the federation.

Amid these apprehensions walks Tengku Abdul Rahman, evenhanded, unperturbed, pointing to the success story that can be enacted in Malaya, rich in rubber, tin, oil palm, copra, and potential industry, strategic in location, if the two races will work in harmony.

"We must introduce a common national education. Our aim is to make everyone federation-minded," says the tengku.

And so he has, by personal example, led the way, adopting his Chinese Meriam and his Malay Sulieman.

After the interview, which took place at his official home on the green hills above Kuala Lumpur, he was seeing to it that Meriam saw an exciting, rollicking American movie that evening.

This is the widely traveled, sophisticated prime minister who studied in England, who at Tokyo in 1958 was elected president of the Asian Football Association (trophies and banners ornament the residence walls), and who made his pilgrimage to Mecca as a devout Moslem to give thanks for independence.

He is a striking, tall, reassuring figure, dressed in Malayan *baju,* or shirt, trousers of the same cream-colored material, and *songkok,* or black cap. He rises early for prayers, later walks downhill alone to his office—in that five-minute solitude sometimes reaching crucial decisions. He is a living example to fellow Asians that the sudden ruler of a brand-new country need be neither emotional, chauvinistic, mercurial, nor suspicious. Around Southeast Asia he is conceded to be "one of the real statesmen of the area."

"I grew up with English boys," he recounts. "There are things you admire in them—their pride in being free people. So you start to want freedom for your own people."

An incident at St. Catherine's College at Cambridge, England, where Abdul Rahman studied, made a deep impression on him—but a more wholesome impression than might have been expected. Students took their turn in living "in" the college, and he applied for the privilege. He was passed by, one year, two years. He inquired why. Finally his tutor said,

"I'll be frank with you; this college is built for Englishmen and we can admit them alone."

"This made me angry," he recalls. "But I thought afterward, 'They are within their rights in excluding me.' Then I carried this a logical step further: 'What right,' I asked myself, 'have Englishmen to rule my country?' "

From there on, the tengku led the fight for Malayan independence, but without bitterness.

"Except for Guinea in Africa, we are the newest nation to achieve independence," he comments. "We are on excellent terms with Britain now—a country which some here disliked very heartily until we had achieved our freedom.

"Because we stand for freedom, we are clearly on the side of the democratic free world. After our experience with the Communists in the jungle fighting, we have banned the Communist party and closed the Chinese Communist bank here."

The prime minister led the delegation which met with Chin Peng, secretary-general of the Malayan Communist party, at Baling in December, 1955, to see if by some kind of generous amnesty the jungle war could be ended. But the Communists would neither abandon their party aims nor their arms.

"Chin Peng convinced me that the Communist aim is to set up a Communist government and nothing less. Thus, coexistence with them is never possible."

As we adjourned to an afternoon tea set on the spacious lawn—a very un-British tea which included such tidbits as *karas,* or shredded rice, which is eaten with milk and sugar much like shredded wheat, *lompang,* or Malayan caramel, and exotically grilled bananas—the prime minister was asked what he considered the most constructive or hopeful domestic development in Malaya. He found it difficult to single out any section of the "forward march" which the federation is beginning in education, industrial development, and all-around expansion.

"We have a five-year plan for development," he said. "We went to the World Bank, the United States, and the sultan of Brunei for loans. We are prepared to grant a tax holiday for five years to new industry. We believe this kind of incentive to private investment should be adopted by all the newly developing countries of Southeast Asia.

"Let's sign a common charter to assure private investment that it can come in, safely."

New schools, meanwhile, are springing up rapidly. A language institute, a residential college at Kota Bharu, two day training colleges, and twelve day training centers have been set up for producing seventeen hundred student teachers annually. There is the Technical College at Kuala Lumpur, the College of Agriculture at Serdang. The University of Malaya is building a brand-new, handsome campus at Kuala Lumpur, where there will be a much-needed Department of Engineering as well as faculties of arts, science, and agriculture.

"I should like to see us working together in development programs with the other nations of Southeast Asia," the prime minister added. "We should have common policies for both economic stability and self-preservation. We have here in Malaya a foreign-exchange advantage in our favor, which could be helpful to the other countries."

Malaya's relations with its neighbors are friendly, and high officials have visited back and forth recently between Indonesia and Malaya.

"What of your relations with Britain?" I asked.

"We owe a lot to the British," he replied, "though before independence we found much to criticize. We owe them thanks for the type of government and civil service they built up here. We owe them for the manner in which independence was achieved, without bloodshed, and for the way they stood by to help us in our new nationhood. And of course for their prodigious help in the jungle battle.

"Indeed," he added with a chuckle, "we keep in close touch with the United Kingdom. We are used to their ways, and to their tricks.

"We should carry on with the lessons learned under the British administration. Why experiment when things are going well?"

Malaya's tin and rubber prospects are improving after a recession-caused slump in prices. New rubber trees are being introduced which actually give a 300 per cent increase in yield, thus improving Malaya's competition with synthetic rubber. The standard of living here is superior to that of neighboring Indonesia, Thailand, or Burma by a considerable degree. There is no serious unemployment. Foreign industry and American banks are reconnoitering Malayan investment prospects. The jungle war is very nearly won.

Some new nations run smack into rugged problems upon achievement of independence. Malaya instead has experienced an exhilarating surge of confidence and common sense.

Before independence, when recruitment for national military service was attempted, whole boatloads of Chinese young men left the country for Communist China. After independence, national service was reintroduced with hardly a ripple of discontent. The prime minister regards this as a small indicium of how freedom can produce positive results.

Malaya is one country where the obvious disagreement between communism and Moslem religion is effective.

"A true Moslem can never be a Communist," reasons the prime minister, "because communism says that you are superstitious if you submit to any power beyond your mortal self."

To sum up, here, then, is a quite remarkable country, presided over by a quite remarkable individual. He received his arts degree in Cambridge as a young man, but returned in 1945 to obtain a law education. He believes in the unifying power of sports, and is promoting an Asian "schoolboy football" tournament. He is tolerant and kindly, but as a close friend says, "he will crack down hard on anybody who makes trouble touting communism—or racialism."

Here is a fledgling nation of which it may accurately be said: "Nothing so became the British rulers as their departure from it." The British did leave behind a well-trained civil service and a workable constitution. They built up the rubber estates and the tin mining whose profits today are financing most of the government's development program. The present Malayan regime is strongly pro-West and has a defense agreement with Britain.

The United States has credited the federation with a modest 10 million dollars from its Development Loan Fund for the improvement of Port Swettenham, seaport for Kuala Lumpur. The World Bank has allotted 110 million dollars for a hydroelectric development in the Cameron Highlands, and the sultan of Brunei in northern Borneo (a very wealthy gentleman) has loaned 100 million dollars from his oil profits for Malaya's rural roads, village improvement, the state university, and the national radio network.

Undeniably Malaya has problems ahead. Its first Parliament

was half elected, half appointed (to represent rubber, tin, industry, and so on). The new elections in the summer of 1959 were expressly designed to bring an all-elected lower house, or Assembly, into being. This is true representative government, and more than one country in free Asia has had trouble making it work. Tengku Abdul Rahman resigned from the government early in 1959 with the fundamental objective of developing his party (the Assembly party composed of Malayan, Chinese, and Indian groupings) into an effective political instrument.

Malaya is truly an oasis of well-being in Asia, with a clean, modern capital city, a brisk atmosphere of newly won independence, and an urge for self-improvement which should make Singapore (an entirely separate city-state harassed by left-wing agitation) look to its laurels. Even so, Peking has not abandoned its designs on this fabulously rich territory and is still trying to stir discontent among Chinese youth, as it has done so successfully in Singapore.

The toughest task ahead will be to persuade the Chinese to abandon their traditional "separateness" and to work for the common goal, a highly prosperous federation. Fortunately, many able business-minded Chinese are cooperating wholeheartedly already in making the new federation effective. Here, if anywhere in Asia, it may be possible to transform a Chinese minority into an indigenous, melded-in group. Malaya is the largest net dollar earner in the Commonwealth, and there is enough material wealth here for all to share.

As for the wealth of brotherhood, the example of Meriam and Sulieman is there for all to see.

16

Kishi

(JAPAN)

Tokyo

JAPAN CAN best serve the world by playing the role of a giant industrial transformer—which changes the high voltage industrialization of America and the West into a lower voltage industrialization which emergent Asia can handle without danger.

This intriguing, if complex, comment tells how Japan's adroit premier, Nobusuke Kishi, sees Japan's central destiny in the challenging years just ahead.

"Japan has proved that the free enterprise system can work in Asia—there is no need to adopt the Communist 'shortcut,' " Mr. Kishi observes. "Now Japan can help the emerging new nations of Asia along the same path."

Premier Kishi has embraced the free enterprise system only in the postwar years. In the 1930's he was a leading exponent of "planned economy" and was the top economic official in the Japanese-controlled state of Manchukuo (Manchuria).

Today he speaks of Japan's destiny chiefly in terms of economic benefits. But it is a role which can be of tremendous importance in combating the future appeal and impact of

Communist China's industrialization, which is rising like a glowering sun over Asia today.

This concept of serving as a giant industrial transformer is a natural one for Japan. This is because Japan's great industrial complex—one of the half dozen largest in the world—operates on both "high voltage" (big factories, big corporations) and "low voltage" (small factories, village and cottage-size industries).

Too many of the emergent, underdeveloped nations of Asia—and elsewhere—want the "big industry" immediately—big steel works, big mills. They will bankrupt their high hopes this way. Primarily small industry, cottage industry, must come first. Japan can supply this small-industry know-how. Japan can be the "economic interpreter" of West to East, in Mr. Kishi's view.

What does Mr. Kishi mean by small industry for Asia? In India I have visited a refugee rehabilitation center where there are a dozen new machines in one large room, none bigger than a small lathe, all "made in Japan." They are machines for splitting, cutting, and machining bamboo. With these superbly operating tools, men can turn heavy bamboo poles into matting, screens, even knitting needles. A Japanese was present at this Calcutta enterprise to show how the machines operated.

Here was a graphic example of a Japanese-engineered small enterprise, using a dozen men. No Detroit assembly line, no mammoth factory required—just twelve men in one room.

Call on Premier Kishi, this slight-figured, affable man in the prime minister's official residence in Tokyo, and you see little about you that suggests Japan's postwar dynamism and potentialities. The offices and waiting rooms are somberly and soberly furnished, and Mr. Kishi carries with him an air of quiet efficiency.

But your exciting experience in threading through Tokyo's teeming city traffic of modern automobiles, trucks, and bicycles, your recent visit to a tremendous and luxurious Japanese department store, and your awareness of the drive and bustle all about you cause you to realize that you are seeing the prime minister of the one nation in all Asia which has approximated Western standards and has even excelled the living standards of some European countries.

"I am convinced that Japan, as a faithful member of the free world, has a useful and constructive role to play in Asia, where the free world faces the challenge of international communism. We are ready to play that role," Mr. Kishi announces.

The danger, as seen by the prime minister of Japan, is that the free nations of Asia—Southeast Asia in particular—are falling behind the general development pace of mankind. To fall behind produces dismay and disorder and opens the gates to communism.

So here is a task for Japan which Mr. Kishi, who has traversed South and Southeast Asia and talked with national leaders there, can be expected to push with singleness of purpose. He is likely to push it as vigorously as another world leader, far around on the other side of the globe, Konrad Adenauer of the West German Republic, has pushed the concept of Germany's inevitable ties to Western civilization.

Mr. Kishi would pioneer new economic ties to link Japan to emergent Asia.

This is a big concept, and one which Mr. Kishi once

carried to Washington in one form—before Washington was prepared to accept the Japanese formula. And—let us be frank—before some of the Southeast Asian nations were certain about Japan's intentions, remembering the days of World War II. Questions of Japanese reparations have had to be settled first, and questions of confidence.

Mr. Kishi is a golfer. He knows the value of the approach shot and the follow-through. He has persevered in his proposal for a coordinated program for the development of Southeast Asia. Now Washington, ready with its own development loan fund, is prepared to listen.

"Asia has risen—to march on the road of progress," Mr. Kishi points out. "How to help realize the hopes and aspirations of Asia is the problem that faces world statesmanship. Japan, as a nation of Asia, has deep sympathy for the aspirations of the Southeast Asian countries to prosperity and progress."

Neither Prime Minister Kishi nor any of his ministers would deny that Japan has a profound self-interest in espousing South and Southeast Asia development. Japan's population will push past the 100 million mark in another ten years or less, despite efforts at population limitation which are bearing some fruit. Japan will need more and more markets for its exports, if it is to keep its burgeoning population employed and fed.

Simultaneously the Japan of 1959 is a marvel of booming production, a welling reservoir of technical know-how of the most advanced and intricate kind. It can manufacture radars, transistor radios, diesel locomotives, industrial power plants, just about everything except the atomic bomb. It can play a most significant role in Asian development—if the Asian countries will allow it to do so.

Asia has some sharp memories of the East Asia Co-Prosperity Sphere which Japan forced upon reluctant peoples before World War II. Today, however, Burma, Thailand, Indonesia, South Viet Nam, Ceylon, India, Pakistan, the Philippines—all could benefit profoundly by Japanese know-how and assistance, if it is as enlightened as Mr. Kishi says it is.

The Tokyo government would not propose that Japan, solely and by itself, undertake the development of Southeast Asia, or that it operate as "transformer" without the "high voltage" coming in from the West. Japan, Mr. Kishi maintains, wants to work in partnership with other highly industrialized nations—with the United States, Britain, West Germany, Canada—in pushing Asian development. Japan already is a member of the Colombo Plan. Japan would step up the pace of this joint activity, with itself playing a larger, more dynamic role therein.

An example of how joint action can produce big results is the recent agreement between Japan and India, whereby Japan will assist India in the development of its iron ore resources and India will export a significant portion of this ore to Japan. Multiply such arrangements in developing other Asian resources—be they jute or cotton, ores or minerals—and one sees what Mr. Kishi has in mind.

Every Japanese high official will admit that Japan must trade to live, and that if a lucrative trade with Communist China should appear feasible, Japan would be sorely tempted. But the warning sign here is that Peking's trade offers are politically motivated, every one of them. Thoughtful Japanese, including the prime minister, know the peril of getting enmeshed in trade agreements and reliances on markets which will be expanded or contracted, squeezed or cozened, to suit Peking's political purposes.

Japanese tend subconsciously to think of China as they knew the mainland back in the 1930's. But, when they are realistic, they are aware that Japan could get dangerously ensnared in a net of Chinese commercial influences. The way to avoid this, Mr. Kishi would aver, is to locate Japan's largest trade interests elsewhere, and that means principally Southeast Asia, since the American market is necessarily of limited size.

"My central concern is to promote steadily improving standards of living in Southeast Asia, through development and trade," Prime Minister Kishi sums up.

Japan's leaders are becoming increasingly aware of the direct economic challenge which Communist China is hurling against all trading nations. Communist Chinese goods—textiles, utensils, even art objects—are being sold in the shops of Hong Kong and Southeast Asia now at prices which undercut Japanese goods. Communist China is becoming the "cheap seller of Asia."

Japanese officials question whether Peking can continue this "dumping" policy permanently—selling goods at prices below cost for the sake of political gain. But the Japanese are resolutely determined to press ahead anyway with blueprints for building a more prosperous free Asia—believing that in the big development programs they will not be outbargained by Communist China.

More immediately, the job is to coordinate plans with Washington, London, and the Colombo Plan capitals, so as to get development programs going. Japan cannot supply very much of the capital. It can supply know-how. It can advise on small-scale industry. It can bring more students to Japan for training in science and engineering and management. It can consume raw materials from the new nations.

Peace and stability these days seem to ride on the wings of adequate economic development. Japan, in its pragmatic, uncoordinated way, has won through to an immense burst of postwar prosperity. Not every nation is prepared to follow its example. India, for instance, prefers a more socialistic solution, with more powerful controls remaining ultimately in the hands of government. But every emergent nation needs the "know-how" of modern industry, and this Japan can supply in abundance.

There are Asians who have had suspicions of Prime Minister Kishi, wondering if his ready smile conceals implacable schemes for economic domination. It is pointed out that, because he held Cabinet office during the war, he was held in Sugamo Prison for three years as a war criminal suspect, though he was never brought to trial.

It is understandable that Japanese liberals shared these doubts and that they were renewed during the parliamentary battle over a government bill to give greater powers to the police. The premier's supporters say the more likely clue to his purposes is found in the fact that following his release from Sugamo in 1948 he entered the business world as comptroller of the Nitto Chemical Industry Company, Ltd. He thinks in terms of industrial progress and promotion.

In Japan the government aids, but does not control, industry. The Liberal-Democratic party of Mr. Kishi aims to expand Japan's essential business of bringing in raw materials, manufacturing them, and exporting the resultant goods. Only thus, Mr. Kishi would say, can Japan survive. This is Japan's essential need in world society.

Premier Kishi has himself visited most of the countries of Southeast Asia. Surprisingly enough, although Japan moved into these countries as a conqueror in World War II, most of them—excepting the Philippines—hold little ill will toward Japan. And even in the case of the Philippines, President Garcia has made a conciliatory trade-and-diplomatic visit to Tokyo. In Indonesia and Burma, for instance, it is accepted as fact that the Japanese gave these lands their major impetus toward freedom by weakening the grasp of the former colonial power.

So a lot of Mr. Kishi's proposal is welcome to the new lands of Asia avidly seeking development programs and foreign aid. Not so welcome would be any implication that these countries should remain, permanently, suppliers mainly of raw materials to more industrially advanced nations like Japan.

It is of course true that Malaya, Indonesia, and other lands rich in raw materials (rubber, tin, oil, copra, for example) will be primarily producing these, and prospering thereby, for a long time ahead. And any industrialization must come gradually, as Mr. Kishi would say, to avoid bankruptcy and dislocation. Still, the Japanese will want to avoid any implication that their Southeast Asian friends are immature or belong in the class of "hewers of wood and drawers of water."

Japan has to work its own passage. It is moving toward a larger independence of the United States. It is seeking to establish new relationships with all the newly emergent countries and ex-colonial lands. It has a precarious job ahead.

Every person in Japan is, as it were, in a common lifeboat.

So long as labor unions do not demand too much, so long as industry makes the right products, this lifeboat will carry the whole 90 million Japanese safely. But factors—waves—beyond Japan can threaten to swamp that lifeboat. It is to Mr. Kishi's credit (his eldest brother was a vice-admiral) that he is scanning the seas, charting the favorable economic currents, watching for shoals.

To him and to his party, Asian development looks like the safest harbor for Japan.

And it is a further credit to Mr. Kishi and the new leadership in Japan—their enlightenment and their perception—that they are offering Japan's assistance on terms of equality among the nations, a pooling of common experience, and a spirit of interdependence which is a far cry from the war lord era of the thirties.

17

Chiang Kai-shek

(REPUBLIC OF CHINA)

Taipei, Formosa

MANY A free-world realist regards Generalissimo Chiang Kai-shek, president of the Republic of China, as a "has been."

Seen on Formosa, sitting ramrod straight for an interview, looking much younger than his years, replying readily and fast, the "Gimo" seems far other than a "has been."

"Our role," he responded emphatically to my question, "is to be a lighthouse of freedom—a beacon of free people giving hope to those who struggle to regain their freedom, in whatever country they may be.

"Our constant effort must be to remain free and ready—so as to hold out hope to others who are in chains."

The generalissimo obviously had in mind Hungary and the Baltic States as well as his own China.

In this Formosa setting, at the end of a long red carpet (from which two attendants had erased our footprints with brooms as we mounted to the Gimo's office), Chiang Kai-shek was impressive and persuasive.

Perhaps it was the fact that Communist China had so recently launched its hideous system of communal living, outdoing Stalin, a system which pointed up the contrast between the free and the police-state China. The Formosa government is amassing a somber dossier on the stark mainland "experiment" of the communes.

Perhaps it was the fact that here, despite some sharp private reservations, the official government view, from Chiang down, was that the Quemoy episode had ended in victory—victory for the Nationalist cause. The Communists had wasted a half million rounds of ammunition, and the Nationalists were still entrenched, weren't they?

Certainly it was evident, as the president talked, that Free China had entered a new phase in its constant struggle against Peking.

"The communes are giving us the opportunity to make crystal clear the night-and-day difference between what we espouse and what the Communists stand for," the generalissimo declared. "They are the last straw. They are totally inhuman—against all human decency and dignity, depriving the individual of every last vestige of his humanity.

"We and the United States are pondering an appeal to the world's conscience, denouncing and condemning this communal experiment."

Three Free China flags stood at attention in a corner of the vast office as the interview, through interpreter Jimmy Chen, went ahead. A picture of Sun Yat-sen, founder of the Chinese Republic, hung over the fireplace. Chinese paintings, some by Madame Chiang, freshened the walls. On the Gimo's desk was a stand of five wood-handled pens and one of those ubiquitous glasses of hot tea found in every Taipei office. The model of a Matador (or more advanced guided missile) stood on a side stand. A bowl of gladioli added to the Oriental touch above the rug of royal blue.

Here sat, one realized suddenly, a symbol of allegiance for Chinese everywhere who resist the writ of Peking, be they among the smart merchants of Hong Kong, the myriad traders throughout Southeast Asia, or the masses on the mainland. There are at present only two symbols for China's future. One is Mao Tse-tung; the other is Chiang Kai-shek. It is as simple as that. Chiang's role is inevitable for him.

"Quemoy was no defeat," the generalissimo continued. "Our effective resistance has profoundly stirred opinion in free Asia, given heart to governments prepared to resist Chinese penetration.

"But the Communists are unpredictable, full of tricks. You can be sure they will not rest after this defeat. They will keep trying, at one point or another, to seize the offshore islands, to move against Formosa, to make trouble at Berlin.

"Whatever they do here, we are confident that we can lick it.

"Their common objective, of course, is to alienate relations between the United States and Nationalist China."

For years General Chiang has been crying that the Communists do not change their ways. Those who have seen evidence of a thaw at Moscow have urged that he qualify his jeremiads. But now that Peking is adopting a super-Stalinist stance, General Chiang's warnings take on somewhat more substance.

The generalissimo has been frustrated in his effort to promote a return to the mainland by force of arms. Now he declares that he is giving much thought to consolidating his bastion of freedom—his "lighthouse"—so that its appeal to the mainland Chinese may be larger and so that its validity as a free nation shall be all the more evident. General Chiang refers questioners on this point to his vice-president and premier, Chen Cheng, who spelled out the projected program to be undertaken by Taipei as follows:

1. On Formosa the "next generation" must be carefully prepared, with good schooling, good life opportunities.

2. The people's standard of living must be raised, which means more manufacturing, more mining, improved agriculture. Land distribution is already an accomplished fact. Some capital developmen programs, such as the Shimen Dam (multipurpose), are already bearing fruit.

3. Finally, the Republic of China should move toward more regional economic cooperation in this part of the world to consolidate the economic strength of nations in Southeast Asia and the Asian island chain. Formosa has already extended technical assistance to South Viet Nam.

"We ought to pool the best ideas of these different countries so as to make better utilization of specialization in solving our common needs," said crisp General Chen Cheng, vice-president. "Our aim is to build up an area where people can enjoy freedom, welfare, democracy, and security."

A big order! And only the beginning of regional collaboration, and not much at that. What course General Chiang steers from now on in his relations with nations other than the United States and Communist China becomes increasingly important.

Obviously both the generalissimo and Vice-President Chen Cheng—an old soldier who once commanded the Third Route Army and later the Burma border area in World War II before becoming chief of staff in 1946—are pleased by the recent changes in government in free Asia and Africa which have put military men and anti-Communists in high office in Pakistan, Burma, Indonesia, and the Sudan.

What did Chiang envisage as Free China's role in regaining the mainland now that a return by force of arms is placed far down the list?

"We foresee a spontaneous uprising on the mainland, as happened in Hungary," he replied. "But Hungary had no outside help. We shall be the outside help—now as well as later. Now we shall develop a combination of political efforts to sustain and to win the hearts and minds on the mainland. Always we shall adhere to the principles of Sun Yat-sen."

He did not spell out the "political efforts," but one assumed they would include flaming appeals in the United Nations against the communes and new, closer diplomatic relations with South Korea, South Viet Nam, Thailand, the Philippines —the anti-Communists of Asia. One assumed this.

The interview was not long when one considers the time consumed by translation. After a half hour the generalissimo stood up, there was a brisk handshake, and it was over. Then came a long walk through the impressive corridors of the Gimo's headquarters, where once sat the Japanese governor of Formosa.

One wonders how many of his new ideas or his old dreams General Chiang now can bring to reality. As he retires to his home on mist-shrouded Grass Mountain, overlooking Taipei, does he believe he can bring about an Asian coalition of anti-Communist nations—either military or economic? Regionalism does not run strong in free Asia, even though Communist China is big and menacing.

Does he really hope for a spontaneous uprising on the mainland, where the overlords carry the machine guns and the exploited millions are unarmed, and where sometimes even the communes improve, temporarily at least, a farmer's lot? Chiang could extend little assistance, because of the vast distances, when lonely Tibet rebelled against Peking. What can Free China do—when Chiang bridles at the "two Chinas" concept, insisting there is only one China, his China, and when many neutralist nations would unthinkingly consign Formosa to Communist China's police state, willy-nilly, and get it over with?

His views have often seemed sternly rigid, as when in his recent book, *A Summing Up at Seventy,* he tut-tuts American economic aid to neutral nations as aiding, he actually contends, the spread of Communist influence. He has fought the Communists for two decades, with his mind fixedly on one subject. Now two of his strongest supporters are gone from Washington's posts of command: Secretary of State John Foster Dulles and Assistant Secretary of State Walter Robertson.

Certainly Chiang has the opportunity, now that Communist China has gone super-Stalinist and now that the schemes of a fighting recovery of the mainland have had to be laid aside, to develop new policies. Can he make Formosa a show window of good government, a rallying point for all Chinese the world over who would topple or moderate the regime at

Peking? Can he make it the offshore West Berlin of the Chinese world, truly the "lighthouse" of which he spoke so eloquently as he began his interview?

One hopes that the generalissimo has vision to see afar as he ponders the changing future from his Grass Mountain aerie.

18

Spaak

(NATO)

Paris

"MR. EUROPE"—alias Paul-Henri Spaak—is now looking for new worlds to conquer, new ways to build sound unity in Europe. Specifically, he would like to see a Common Europe parliament trumpeted into session, based on universal suffrage.

Specifically again, he would like to see the Common Market extended to embrace many more European nations than the original six.

Who is this man who so naturally and acceptably wears the title "Mr. Europe"? How looks the future to this former Belgian premier and foreign minister, whose dynamic advocacy has had so much to do with—

> The Benelux Union,
> The Council of Europe,
> The Coal-Steel Community,
> The European Defense Community,
> Euratom,
> The Common Market,
> The political side of NATO?

Take a taxi to the Palais de Chaillot, in the shadow of the Eiffel Tower, and walk into the vast creaky-floored, temporary structure which now houses the North Atlantic Treaty Organization offices in Paris.

In an inner sanctum, relaxed beside a paper-strewn desk, you meet a stocky, rotund figure who physically reminds one distinctly of that other enunciator of Pan-Europeanism—Sir Winston Churchill. M. Spaak is officially active here today as NATO's secretary-general. But his ideas, his enthusiasm, his persuasions, have been operating all along the European front.

"I am convinced that the future belongs to the great human communities," he explains simply. "Europe is one of these communities."

M. Spaak has been wrestling, this past year, with the problem of building some degree of political coordination into a military aggregate, NATO—instilling a habit of consultation among the members. It has been no easy assignment, though progress has been registered.

Economic coordination is showing more spectacular results, so far, with the launching of the Common Market and Euratom.

But "Mr. Europe" is not satisfied to leave it at that.

"If in the political field we could have a European parliament!" he muses. "A parliament that would be based on universal suffrage. People are beginning to study this question —for the six countries of the Common Market.

"I believe that the whole concept of the European community is taking hold, is growing, in the minds of Europeans, particularly since the launching of the Common Market in January."

A kind of European parliament meets annually at Strasbourg, in the Council of Europe. Its members are, however, named by the associated governments or parliaments, not elected by ordinary citizens all across Europe. M. Spaak's idea may be visionary; yet a dozen years ago how many could have foretold today's integration strides?

European unity moves on against old and new currents of opposition, against recurrent nationalism in France, and against the constant Soviet challenge.

"Do you believe that Moscow is still a threat to Western Europe—to NATO or otherwise?" I asked.

"The Soviet challenge is today thought to be mainly economic," M. Spaak replied. "But let me say that the fact the Communists should be developing their productivity and becoming rich doesn't strike me as something bad. I feel that a rich Communist is probably less to be feared than a poor Communist.

"What we must realize is that the Communist goal is not merely an economic or a social threat; it is much wider; the ambition of communism is to be the wellspring of a new civilization, in which the essential foundations of our spiritual, intellectual, moral, and political life will be challenged.

"Our whole spiritual inheritance, which is, after all, our most important possession, is threatened by this system which claims to be a universal doctrine borne on the tide of history."

Although M. Spaak has been a socialist and a free thinker throughout his life, he has the same vigorous distaste for communism felt by most Western European socialists, whether that distaste is based on Christian or on humanist grounds.

"The Communists cite statistics to show they will catch up with us," he adds with a twinkle. "But I note that Khrushchev has been stating lately that Malenkov's statistics were erroneous. I hope his are better.

"At best, they will merely show that the Communists have caught up, economically, to where we were—yesterday."

Indeed, as M. Spaak surveys the Western European scene from Paris—and he is quite a surveyor, an "idea man"—he sees this continent facing great opportunity, and great responsibility.

There is, for instance, the need to keep NATO up to the mark militarily in a time of rapidly changing military science and guided missiles. NATO defenses are still vital. But the Soviet military threat to Western Europe was blunted, he believes, a few years after the Atlantic alliance came into being. It is still blunted, he argues.

Today NATO is reaching beyond military preparadeness, setting up habits of political and economic cooperation, even as its "committee of three wise men" (a Canadian, a Norwegian, and an Italian) had recommended in 1956. This eminently suits M. Spaak, who is a practicing politician at heart.

"Public opinion hardly appreciates yet the new amount of consultation among the fourteen member states that goes on," says the secretary-general. "For example, in the first nine months of 1958 our permanent council held some seventy 'special' meetings, dealing with political problems—Berlin, Cyprus, the Rapacki Plan—in addition to its normal weekly sessions.

"Just the other day, in one of these restricted sessions, what did we discuss? The situation in Berlin. We also heard a report on the two conferences taking place in Geneva, on nuclear tests and surprise attacks. Owing to lack of time, mind you, we were not able to listen to one delegate who had promised a report on Middle Eastern problems. We heard the regular report by the United States delegate on the Far East.

"So you see, in the Atlantic Council, we discussed international problems facing the whole of the free world; we were not restricted to Europe.

"Public opinion may know only that the NATO authorities by themselves failed to find a solution to the thorny Cyprus issue which was straining relations between three of our members, Britain, Greece, and Turkey.

"What people do not realize is that the very fact that Cyprus was tackled within the NATO alliance is proof that public opinion is more and more demanding that NATO handle problems outside its original mandate. NATO is becoming a forum where all kinds of politico-diplomatic problems come to be settled."

NATO is not the only organization where expansion is or should be the order of the day, M. Spaak holds. The "six nations"—West Germany, France, Italy, Belgium, the Netherlands, Luxembourg—have developed several strands of unification, but others should join them, he would say, and of course he refers to the prospects—not overly bright at the moment—of expanding the Common Market into a free-trade area embracing Britain and the Scandinavian countries as well.

"But those who wish to join 'the six' must share the burdens, too," M. Spaak says. "For example, in our original Rome treaty setting up the Common Market a European investment bank was organized, for investments in underdeveloped areas—and a fund was set up for African development. More use should be made of these.

"Then take foreign aid. Western European nations, combining forces, could make vast contributions to the economies of the emerging countries. Some nations have done much, individually. They could do more, acting together."

But with all these hopeful omens, there is a serious challenge now visible on Western Europe's horizon—and it is the challenge of resurgent nationalism, particularly in today's French leadership.

Some experts, viewing the scene with alarm, are asking if "the men who follow" Adenauer in Germany and de Gaulle in France may not prefer to unscramble the Common Market, dismantle the Coal-Steel Community, weaken the ties of NATO, and return to a fitful and uncertain "cooperation-by-government" which, in fact, opens the way to deadly economic rivalry and eventually political rivalry.

How does M. Spaak—who suffered one major defeat at the hands of the nationalists when the European Defense Community was scuttled by the French Parliament—feel about the "new nationalism"?

"In certain European countries," he replies, "and particularly in France since de Gaulle, there has been a definite revival of nationalist sentiment, yes. But I do not believe that this revival sounds the knell of our hopes.

"Nationalism does not exclude the 'European sense.' "

M. Spaak admitted that perhaps Premier Michel Debré, Jacques Soustelle, and some few others might seek to reverse France's economic integration. Others suggest that France will continue its ties to NATO and the Common Market only if other nations support its North African policies.

"From what I observe of West Germany and Italy, nationalistic feelings there are not in any way opposed to European feelings. For example, I find the European ideas of German

Defense Minister Strauss, whom I knew at Strasbourg, to be most acceptable."

There are, fortunately, many allies to the "European" cause. There are other workers in the vineyard, from France, West Germany, and Britain. And the United States is always standing by to do what it can to promote the kind of economic federation that made a prosperous single market of the American continent.

Meanwhile, to M. Spaak, every step toward greater consultation, cooperation, cultural ties, trade ties, scientific knowledge-sharing, defense pooling, or tariff reduction is all to the good.

An idealistic European but also a very practical politician, M. Spaak does not insist on perfectionism. He is pleased at NATO's strides toward consultation among members—pleased that, when the president of the United States writes to Mr. Khrushchev, he first shows a copy of his letter even to the premier of Luxembourg. But he does not expect NATO will be able to unify Anglo-American policies on Communist China, for example.

Once an advocate of Belgian neutrality who almost joined King Leopold in the Belgian surrender of World War II, M. Spaak now is an internationalist who has no use for neutrality. He feels the European countries are too small to play significant roles today and must combine in a "united states of Europe." Only thus can, say, his own land of Belgium maintain its well-being.

As a younger man, M. Spaak led street demonstrations supporting his political principles. The cause of European unity —which is given cold scrutiny at times by the Ruhr industrialists and the French chauvinists—needs support from outspoken rough-and-tumble politicians like this Belgian. Otherwise the general public may never come to realize that the long-term advantages greatly outweigh the short-term hardships.

Of the Common Market and Euratom proposals he once said: "There must be success here; this is Europe's last chance."

This could be true.

19

Hammarskjold

(UN)

United Nations

HOW SHALL mankind learn to live together? When all the hopes and anxieties of a score of political leaders, and their peoples, have been expressed—the aspirations, the tensions, the claims and counterclaims, the bare-knuckle challenges—how can reconciliation within the family of man begin?

Dag Hammarskjold, secretary-general of the United Nations, has an answer.

"The UN stands for man," he says, simply. "Here—more than anywhere else—the slow, painstaking process goes forward, step by step."

Go see this engaging, unpretentious "practical intellectual" in the slightly rarified, spacious atmosphere of the thirty-eighth floor of the UN building (the glass house where people must not throw stones) and you say to yourself: This man speaks with vast yet simple eloquence of the patient, oft-criticized business of the UN. He clearly understands its aims, problems, what is practically possible, what must await further growth.

Veritably, if one may lapse into Americanese jargon, he is "Mr. United Nations" himself.

So you ask this son of a former Swedish prime minister, belonging to a line of officials who have served Sweden with distinction since 1610, what he regards as the most hopeful development at the UN today. Mr. Hammarskjold quickly replies:

"It is the growing use of the techniques and instrumentalities of the UN for quiet negotiation and diplomacy, for the unpublicized, serious mediation of disputes—away from the forums of debate, with no votes taken, just the meeting of minds.

"We are still experimenting with the techniques and instrumentalities of this private, or quiet, diplomacy."

The earnest, backstage, informal talks which brought about the placing of the UN Emergency Force on the Egypt-Israel boundary are a successful instance of this quiet diplomacy.

In quite another field, there is the admirable functioning of that UN committee of nuclear scientists—including governmental representatives from the United States, Britain, and the Soviet Union—which made the daily, unpublicized, fundamental decisions that paved the way for the first Geneva "atoms for peace" conference in 1955, and the second in 1958.

"This quiet diplomacy can work for big disputes or little," comments the secretary-general.

"But too often the dispute is dumped on us as a last resort, when the fat is already very near the fire.

"I'd like to see the instrumentalities for negotiation of the UN put into use as a natural habit, and not so sporadically as now."

Why is the UN needed to supplement bilateral negotiations or some more limited forum?

"All the varied interests and aspirations of the world meet here upon the common and persuasive ground of the Charter. There are, thus, unique opportunities for diplomacy to bring different viewpoints closer together and to make progress, little by little, toward solutions which reflect the general interest and principles of the Charter."

The secretary-general dealt in lofty concepts, yet one had the solid impression that he espoused no idealism which he had not already glimpsed in at least limited operation, and successful operation, in the halls of the UN.

"You see," he continued, "we have reached a time when Churchill's colorful phrase about the UN—that it's 'jaw-jaw instead of war-war'—can be seen as an oversimplification.

"This is not only a town meeting of the world. It's not only a world forum, though that continues to be an important function. It's beginning to become also, I hope, a quiet room to which the nations can come for the quiet settling—or at least taking the wind out—of their disputes, by patient diplomatic processes."

The slight Swedish accent added to the charm of his conversation. Here was the secretary-general, who had traveled frequently to the Middle East to damp down tempers, who had flown to Communist China to obtain release of American fliers, who had made extensive world tours, visiting trouble spots.

While people talked about establishing a UN "presence" in Jordan, or Gaza, here was the central "presence" in New

York quietly, tenaciously speaking for the methods of conciliation. Listening, you could almost palpably touch—

The calming influence of the UN,
The voice of reason enunciated in its Charter,
The impetus toward peace felt by billions of people,
The obvious interdependence among mankind.

We turned to new subjects. How did Mr. Hammarskjold view the significant increase in the membership—hence the General Assembly voting power—of the Asian and African nations? Was this weighting the UN dangerously on the side of inexperience and perhaps of hostility toward the West?

"No, indeed," he replied. "We are in a period of great adjustment in world affairs.

"The newly emergent countries belong in the world picture. To help guide their adjustment in peaceful ways, it is just as important to the West as to them that they be given a voice in the UN, and a vote. Nor should we forget that many of the newly independent countries spring from great and ancient civilizations. The Assembly should, as nearly as possible, represent the whole family of man.

"In this connection, it is sometimes said, as a criticism, that the smaller nations generally have a voice in the UN out of proportion to their responsibilities. Well, we have all seen failures to act responsibly in international life, but these failures have been among the great as well as the small nations. In the UN, the voice of the smaller nations may often be closer to that of the man in the street, to world opinion, than the voice of the big powers, which unfortunately is more likely to be filtered, shall we say, by the necessities of prestige and power. Furthermore, the smaller powers have frequently made important and highly responsible diplomatic contributions toward reaching agreements in the UN."

But what of the shrill and "politicized" debate which frequently goes on at the UN, with delegates simply scoring debating points off each other, or making dull speeches for home consumption?

"Oh," exclaimed the secretary-general, "let them speak to their constituents now and then! Every member of a Parliament or Congress must do so at times.

"However, for the long-range future, a more effective and increasing use of the entire UN as a diplomatic instrument, in which even the functions of debate and vote are used more frequently to further a diplomacy of reconciliation in the sense of the Charter rather than merely to score propaganda points, or to defend against them, offers the best hope for a peaceful evolution in the relationship of Asia and Africa with the West. Indeed, in the same way it should improve the relationships of the West with the Communist countries."

It is well known that Mr. Hammarskjold favors the funneling of more foreign-aid and development programs through the UN, and is delighted at the modest growth in the use of the UN's multilateral agencies for dispensing technical assistance and financial investment to underdeveloped areas, as, for instance, the new UN Special Fund.

What advantages did he see in the multilateral approach?

"A UN aid program has no political strings attached," he replied. "Through UN auspices the wealthy and heavily industrialized can assist the underdeveloped with fewer political tensions or complications.

"You realize that it is sometimes more difficult to receive than to give. Under a multilateral system, in a world where we all share our common fate, it reflects on no one's dignity when aid is proffered or accepted."

But now that mankind was making sudden, vast breakthroughs in physics, fabricating cataclysmic nuclear weapons, and daring to probe into outer space, could the UN hope to cope with this challenge, too?

"There is actually great hope as well as great danger here," Mr. Hammarskjold replied. "The new scientific advances—the peaceful utilization of atomic energy for power generation, for instance—hold out the possibility that problems that would have broken our backs previously can be solved—problems such as that posed by the rapid increase in world population, which thus far has eaten up most of the economic advances of the newly developing countries.

"There's much to be done, in problems of control, of course. The goal of disarmament seems as far away as ever, and we must continue to make new efforts for some progress, like those that have been made in the Geneva talks on nuclear weapons tests and surprise attacks.

"Note, however, the gains in international cooperation in the peaceful uses of atomic energy. We have caught the ball at the beginning of its flight. That didn't happen at the time of the Industrial Revolution. We have broken up secrecy early, we have installed world-recognized safety measures, we have promoted wide exchange of scientific information. This is a very good beginning."

Quiet diplomacy, patience, a constant seeking of the common denominator of agreement, a constant probing for conciliation and reconciliation—these are quite evidently Dag Hammarskjold's methods of operation.

They are sometimes criticized by one side or the other, as when the UN observers found so little evidence of infiltration of arms and fighters across the Syrian-Lebanese border. Or as when the secretary-general promptly returned the Gaza Strip to Egyptian administration after the Israeli withdrawal was completed in March, 1957. But the Lebanese border now is quiet. And the Gaza side of the Armistice Demarcation Line is still patrolled effectively by the 5,400-man UN Emergency Force.

"Remember," said the secretary-general, "we have established there a peace patrolling force, not a military fighting force. It is there by agreement and consent. It is not and cannot be the kind of army to enforce peace that, under the Charter, could only be created by the Security Council with all the great powers agreeing. But its presence has proved to be a very important contribution to peace in the area. Since Suez, in Lebanon and Jordan, we have found that other forms of a UN presence can help in tense situations. In Lebanon it took the form of the UN Observation Group—not quite six hundred officers and technicians acting as air and ground observers.

"In Jordan it has taken the form of a special representative of the secretary-general, assisted by a small administrative staff. Thus, experience so far has shown that, depending on each special case, the UN may be called on to send from one man to more than five thousand men to help meet, by peaceful means, situations dangerous to peace. The need for flexibility in planning for future emergencies is therefore apparent."

What was the fundamental lesson to be learned at the UN, Mr. Hammarskjold, former deputy foreign minister of Sweden, was asked.

"The UN teaches everybody that the world's great issues are not all black and white—not just bad people on one side and good people on the other. And the nations' representatives here learn this, too.

"When you, as a delegate, discover how your opponent ticks, what motivates him, then you can build up professional relationships which are more constructive.

"If you know foreign minister X sufficiently well to see his problems from his side, you henceforth will deal more effectively with him, and more thoughtfully, than if you have only a cartoonist's image of him.

"The world is complex and there are many different temperaments, ambitions, past histories, dogmas, and dialectics. Today they all convene at the UN, with their ambitions and jealousies, hopes and strivings.

"But there are very few fanatics here," observed Mr. Hammarskjold. "Even the toughest dialecticians are susceptible to the influence of the UN. Here at these sessions we become accustomed to the two-sided approach, you know.

"Give us time. Give us years. The UN is not a world government. It is a framework for diplomatic operations.

"As I said to the members of the British Parliament last April, 'It is because world community does not exist at a time when world interdependence has become a reality that world organization has become a necessity as a bridge which may help us to pass safely over this immense period of transition.'

"Here we maintain contacts across difficult frontiers, a

forum for discussion, a schoolroom for the future, and above all, an assortment of instruments and techniques for reconciliation.

"Here the most constructive forces in international life can find increasing expression."

20

Nehru

(INDIA)

New Delhi

THE SENSITIVE, mobile, thoughtful face—and that small touch of elegance, the rosebud in the third buttonhole of the high-collared *achkan!* This is Prime Minister Nehru—and so much more is Nehru—sitting across from you, at his marvelously wide desk in India's red sandstone Secretariat Building.

Perhaps the most influential Asian of our time. Spokesman for 400 million Indians and many other "uncommitted" peoples. High-born Brahmin, educated at Harrow and Cambridge, who early embraced Gandhi's independence movement. Mainstay of India's Congress party and indeed of India's whole democratic approach. Giver (as he once wrote concerning Gandhi) of "clear and pointed expression to the vaguely felt ideas of the age."

I wish that many persons, including those who criticize him, could sit here and watch that intuitive aristocratic face light up, could see mobile thought take expression, could hear his concepts firsthand. But I would not wish too many interviewers on Mr. Nehru, for when we arrived his countenance seemed weary and burdened.

But he liked the questions asked, and was immediately engaged in animated replies.

In brief summary:

1. Jawaharlal Nehru believes that the most exciting thing under way in India today is the education of women. This release of the feminine thought is changing the social fabric of India.

2. India's central role in world affairs, as he sees it, is to lessen tensions by promoting peaceful discussion and a step-by-step growth in understanding between the great powers.

3. India's further role among the underdeveloped nations—implicit in the two five-year plans nearly completed and the third plan with which Mr. Nehru is now wrestling—is to prove that a backward nation can modernize itself under the democratic system, and need not embrace the police-state methods of communism.

Mr. Nehru rises at 6:15 A.M. and by 8:30 has done thirty minutes of yoga exercise, including a headstand, eaten breakfast, read five morning papers, glanced at cables, fed his two pet pandas. At 8:30 he meets specially with peasants, workers, hillsmen, whoever throngs his office. Throughout the day he confers with government officials, bobs up and down in Parliament, has a guest for lunch, inspects projects—and may be at his desk until midnight.

When he speaks of retiring, the Congress party declares it cannot do without him. He has a hand in every Indian venture, has chartered India's social democratic ideology, determines its daily foreign policy. He is affectionately regarded throughout the length and breadth of India. All sorts of world leaders

—Khrushchev, Tito, Chou En-lai, Diefenbaker, the Dalai Lama—have beaten a path to his door.

As he sat in his "foreign office," not far from the Parliament Building from whose floor he occasionally "lectures" the world, he wore the usual brown homespun, high-buttoned *achkan,* a kind of morning coat, white trousers, and as always he had tucked a pink rosebud into the third buttonhole of his coat. He donned his white Gandhi cap only when, after the interview, we adjourned to the warm sun of the balcony for photographs.

Because Prime Minister Nehru so interestingly enunciated his answers, because he so carefully set forth India's "uncommitted" but positive role in world affairs, and because I took such complete notes, this interview will be largely verbatim question and answer. Mr. Nehru spoke very much as follows:

Q.: Mr. Prime Minister, every country today has some essential role that it can or should play in world affairs. What do you, sir, envisage as India's central role, its individual destiny in the world scene?

A.: Our policy is to try to be helpful, to try to bring nations at length to the point of peaceful discussion, step by step.

Take the disarmament problem. All of us want peace, all peoples do. But we are in a highly complicated situation in which nations are governed by fear. The West fears a heavily armed Soviet Union; Russia fears a rearmed Germany. So—they dare not take a step to weaken their own strength.

It is a question, then, of improving the psychological approach. We try by our policy to lessen tensions, to initiate quiet discussions, new approaches, so the arms problem may be decided a little more easily.

Now, of course, all our past experience is against one country dominating another. We felt strongly on this, for instance, concerning France in Algeria. But even there we do not go about running down France. We express ourselves in friendly terms to France, hoping that its tradition of liberty will enable it to find the solution.

Running down a country creates strong reactions. You don't open men's minds by running them down. So you do things mildly. It's a question of approach.

Q.: You have been accused, or India has been accused, Mr. Prime Minister, of being neutralist, so neutralist as not to take firm stands on great issues. Do you see it a different way?

A.: Our foreign policy is inevitably conditioned by our past. We had a severe struggle with Britain, but we avoided running down the British. We did speak out strongly against injustices, but even at the height of that struggle the amount of ill will was remarkably small. Britons could still walk safely among our crowds. This was the result of years of conditioning by Gandhi.

["Go to any continent and you find India's name associated with peace," Mr. Nehru told Parliament the next day, amid applause. "What India has said has found an echo in many countries."]

From a practical point of view, when it is obvious that war would bring total destruction, it becomes essential to avoid war. Therefore it becomes illogical to heat up the atmosphere. The cold war is not a suitable thing to have if we would avoid the hot war.

Now this does not mean a surrender of principles. But we avoid the atmosphere of hostility. One doesn't see any other way.

[India and Mr. Nehru are proud that twice India has been asked by the United Nations to help settle conflicts: in Korea and in Indo-China.]

You mustn't, of course, lay down your arms and weaken yourself. But in taking positions, do it rather quietly. Methods of constant verbal attack do not help at all. Any great power can by military pressure and threats induce a smaller country to alter its policy. But when both countries are big and powerful, threats just do not work.

Q.: How do you view the new policy lines in both Moscow and Peking? Does this make the conciliatory approach more difficult?

A.: Where rigidity grows, that indeed becomes a barrier. Despite recent disputes, however, I see a greater approach to settling down on the part of Moscow. Every great revolution upsets the life of a country, but eventually it settles down. Unfortunately after the Soviet revolution a continuous series of events kept the Soviet from settling down: the civil war, two world wars, the feeling of being surrounded or in a state of siege.

These developments prevented any approach to normality. Today we do see in the Soviet Union a reduction of the police apparatus and other hopeful signs. Back of Soviet behavior is fear, and the conditioning of forty years. The Russians personally are a very friendly people.

Q.: But what of Communist China?

A.: China is in the full flood of revolution—has been undergoing revolution for a hundred years, actually. Now the process moves at a considerable pace. The sheer numbers are overwhelming. China's rulers believe they must prevent their people from relaxing discipline; otherwise China's problems would overwhelm the present rulers. Of course there is a considerable degree of rigidity in China's outlook toward the external world —a lack of experience and knowledge concerning the rest of the world.

Now China is setting up a colossal system of communes, seeking a vast increase in agricultural production. They are also establishing what might be called "cottage factories" for production of pig iron. We have been seeking as much information as possible about this drive, sending in teams to see what is going on.

One thing is certain, they are working very hard. Concerning these communes—I just don't know. I would object to being regimented so much.

Normally, these big revolutions go ahead, and then back, and finally some equilibrium is obtained. The great problem of a country like China is how far they have uprooted themselves from their past—from the old broad Chinese outlook on life. Will the old roots reappear?

In the Soviet Union there have been vast changes, yet during and after the war there has been some return to nationalism. Whether this is helpful or not I don't know, but it intrigues me.

I have a desire to change India, for instance, but not to uproot it from its past. Something of value is acquired by a nation in its development—in its progress through millenniums of history.

Q.: You speak of development and progress in modern India, Mr. Prime Minister. What do you regard as the most hopeful, the most encouraging domestic development in India today? What encourages you most?

A.: Yesterday I attended the university convocation here in Delhi. There were nearly a thousand young women graduates. That kind of thing is happening in varying degrees all over India. There were two doctors of philosophy, there were masters of arts—all women; they are highly trained. Throughout India, the number of girls in school has increased greatly.

Now, that is basic. Ultimately, education is the greatest liberating factor in a country. The education of women has even greater influence on society than the education of men. Women here have been more tied to old tradition than men. And they exert a powerful influence in home life. So this education is having a powerful effect on the whole social approach in India.

We enacted legislation recently to give equality to women in marriage, inheritance, and divorce. This was a brave thing to do—against the tradition of two thousand years or more. That too has had a liberating influence on women. It is not, of course, 100 per cent implemented as yet.

Another hopeful development is our effort to put an end to untouchability. This, too, takes time. But even by daily practice this is proceeding. In modern life—in factory, tramcar, railway carriage—there is no room for untouchability. This is a liberating factor on those who were by social custom suppressed; they don't put up with it.

Q.: Would you single out other encouraging factors?

A.: Yes, thirdly, I would list the stress we have laid on the development of science. Ten years ago, right after independence was achieved, our effort was to set up big national laboratories—where thousands of men and women would be working. All of this leads to influencing mental attitudes and ways of thinking.

Our country's drive against poverty has not always suc-

Spaak *Converse*

Converse **Hammarskjold**

Nehru *Converse*

Converse **Diefenbaker**

ceeded in the massive way that we wanted it to succeed. It is not merely a question of more roads, more hospitals. The test is how far the people themselves take these things in hand and run them themselves. Does what we do take the people out of their ruts and grooves of life?

We have had some success with our village programs; considering the recent start, it has spread remarkably. It covers over 300,000 out of 550,000 villages—more than half. The results have been good but we are not quite satisfied. The effort should be not to rely on official agencies, but to pull up the roughly 300 million rural inhabitants and make them really self-reliant.

So we stress village councils and village cooperatives. We stick to small-sized organizations because we feel that this helps in the development of self-reliance. In a big organization a man is lost; some official bosses it. In a village, they know each other like a family. Men will do more for a village.

Our biggest problem is, of course, food production, and the need is to develop better farming techniques.

Q.: Could we turn again to foreign affairs, Mr. Prime Minister—and to the criticism sometimes leveled at India, that it has not allied itself with the West, which is seeking to deter aggression? You do not believe, I know, that India should sign on the dotted line, to obtain foreign aid or for any reason.

A.: If we were to sign on the dotted line, that would be no assurance to you. When you are dealing with a specific government of a country, and that government takes action which is unpopular, then you are unpopular. Whereas, if in a socially backward country you help, say, in land reform, then you promote self-reliance and stability.

["Some people say our policy is that of sitting on the fence," the prime minister told India's Parliament the following day. "It is not. . . . It is a policy inherent in the mental outlook of India. It is a mere accident of fate that I have represented that policy. . . .

"We cannot say that there are only two ways of action in this world today. If you say that, then you have to join, at least mentally, one side or the other.

"The possession of great armed might, or great financial power, doesn't necessarily make a country wiser. If I have an atom bomb that doesn't mean I am wiser."]

Q.: Is there an added predatory ingredient, which is not merely fear or rigidity, in "international communism" which makes one side—one bloc—today more difficult to deal with?

A.: The problems of today would be better understood if we thought of them more often in terms of power politics rather than exclusively as communism versus anticommunism. By using these terms we obscure realities. If Communist China and the Soviet Union had not gone communist, they would still be formidable nations.

It is true, of course, that communism is a proselytizing creed —in history there have been others. Gradually they toned down and began to live more largely in the realm of coexistence, even while still proselytizing. The same expectation is possible here. It may be that we shall see an intervening stage of conflict and half-conflict. But even the proselytizing, or gaining of greater influence, cannot be achieved today by war. So you limit it to other influences, as, to success in economic fields. This, at least, is not war.

When the interview was completed, we walked out onto a sunny balcony for photographs by Gordon Converse. Then the prime minister returned to his long day of work. One of his most urgent coming conferences with other government leaders concerned India's third five-year plan. India is able to complete its second ambitious five-year plan thanks to generous infusions of loans and credits from the West—the United States, Canada, West Germany, Britain. With Communist China seeking swift industrialization via the police-state imposition of the commune, surely it is in the West's interest that India should succeed by the democratic methods it has adopted.

Suppose you drive from Delhi to the Himalaya foothills, as I did, and see the huge Bhakra Dam a-building. You say to yourself, "This is good." Impounded monsoon waters will irrigate 10 million acres and sluice hydroelectric power to new as-yet-unbuilt chemical, cement, and aluminum plants.

Then drive about the new oil refineries at Bombay and the new factories there and you conclude, "India's industrial base is coming along."

But then you thread through bullock-cart traffic on northern roads, and you realize how densely populated is southern India, including the state of Kerala, where a Communist government was elected to power. And you learn that India still has a chronic food grain shortage of 1.5 million tons annually—and you finally ask: "Can India really make it?"

Can India indeed prove that industrial modernization and agricultural reform and the whole colossal task of moving an unwieldy peasant-based state into the twentieth century will be accomplished by democratic methods? Communist China is moving ahead by drastically authoritarian techniques. Can India do it while preserving civil liberties?

This is the oft-stated challenge. But it becomes real and poignant and vital here in New Delhi when you see Nehru and his government wrestling with the goals and objectives—and stark needs—of India's third five-year plan.

For India must indeed move forward with a third in 1961-62, and a fourth after that. The factories below the Bhakra Dam must be built. Unemployment must diminish in Kerala. Somehow the chronic food shortage must end despite an annual increase in population. Resettlement of 9 million refugees from Pakistan—taking place almost overnight—must be completed.

What's to be done? India can project a "bold" third five-year plan and maintain the headway now gained. Or it can decrease its pace of modernization and risk political disaster—and the advent of a more authoritarian form of government.

The point which must be of major interest to the United States and the West is that India's third plan must have major infusions of foreign aid or it will falter and fail. One authority estimates that the United States will need to underwrite the last two years of the second five-year plan and the five years of the third (ending in 1966) to the tune of 3 billion dollars—plus larger allocations of surplus food grains.

Would this big underwriting—with other Western industrialized countries doing their part—be worth while? Is it in our own enlightened self-interest? Is there value and virtue in the commitment expressed by the Kennedy-Cooper Senate amendment to "see India through"?

There is intense interest throughout free Asia in development programs of all sorts. The Communist China experiment is being watched carefully. If democratic India were to stumble and fall, and Peking, with Moscow's assistance, were to succeed, there is not the slightest doubt that the repercussions would be tremendous. The United States has seen one of Asia's great nations go communist; it would be cataclysmic if the second great populous nation went the same way.

Congress should consider the potentialities. It would be useful if it could decide this year how big a stake it ought to have here. Then India's five-year planners would have a sounder base for their blueprinting.

Then, with other Western powers sharing the investment load, a longer-range program could be worked out so that too much debt repayment would not fall due during the critical years just ahead. India could decide how much effort to expend in the next "forward leap" on engineering and secondary industries, and how much on land reform, cooperatives, village improvement, and the whole complicated drive to boost India's agricultural output.

To Americans it should be worth a great deal to have a share in proving to Asia and to the entire watching world that communism does not offer to backward countries the only road into the twentieth century.

21

Diefenbaker

(CANADA)

Ottawa

THE TALL, brisk man with the alert blue eyes and the ripple of curly gray hair strode through the double door to greet us.

"No secretaries or clerks here yet," the prime minister of the third largest geographical area on earth said without formality. "Come in and let's talk."

It was very early (8 A.M.) in the East block of Canada's high Houses of Parliament, set majestically on a windy bluff above the dark current of the Ottawa River. Northward the forested hills stretched far away to the horizon and beyond —even to Hudson Bay.

But John George Diefenbaker is used to rising early. Frequently he has put in two hours of work at home before his office formally opens at 9 A.M.

We gathered ourselves around an uncluttered desk, beneath the fireplace portrait of Sir John Macdonald, Canada's first prime minister, who had first strung the disparate provinces together by subsidizing the Canadian Pacific Railroad.

Few nations on earth have as bright prospects as Canada has. Untapped wealth. Strapping energy. Hewing to the old tales, one might say up here that it is as though Paul Bunyan of the fantastic frontiersman strength had gone to college and won a Phi Beta Kappa key of learning, had traded Babe the Blue Ox for an industrial laboratory, and is now in business in a big way and becoming known throughout the world community as a highly respected, public-spirited fellow.

Prime Minister Diefenbaker himself had, clearly, pondered the meaning of this "new" Canada.

"What is Canada's most significant development today? Surely it is this dynamic new concept of Canadianism," Mr. Diefenbaker mused. "It is a feeling of unity, and it is a sense of destiny, an awareness of what Canada can contribute in this churning world.

"Canada has not felt this to the same degree since the years immediately following confederation in 1867."

Outside, Canada's Parliament clock, so closely resembling London's Big Ben, soon struck eight-fifteen. Across town in the famed Rideau Club, where members of Cabinet and Parliament gather and converse in English and in French, talk later that day might dwell on the prime minister's recent "Commonwealth tour," which included not only Britain, Pakistan, India, Ceylon, Malaya, Australia, and New Zealand, but also visits with Britain's Macmillan, France's de Gaulle, West Germany's Adenauer, and Italy's premier. It was a revealing, impressive trip.

One recalled a wise Ottawa newsman's estimate of Mr. Diefenbaker: "He intends to become a world statesman. He intends to make his mark. You'll see."

One could well believe, in the crisp, zippy air of the north, that a Canadian hour for greatness had struck. And that Canada had a prime minister who was "up before breakfast" to meet that hour.

It is indeed a propitious time for Canada. The "Dominion" —it seldom uses that term any more—is developing powerfully as a nation. Its population has risen to 17 million—4.5 million just since World War II. Its industries are leapfrogging ahead. It is dispatching railways, highways—and prospectors flying airplanes—to pry open the mineral-rich northlands.

Its opposition leader in Parliament has won a Nobel Prize. Its suburbs in Edmonton, Calgary, and points west are booming as new petro-chemical plants sprout on the prairies.

And in the midst of this, the voters have given Mr. Diefenbaker a resounding mandate. His Progressive-Conservatives won 208 seats in Parliament, and the combined opposition only 57. It is the largest number of seats ever held by a single party in Canada. It was an earned triumph, by a man who spoke for "Canadianism." And it was a very far cry from the days when candidate Diefenbaker was defeated twice in bids to sit in the Saskatchewan Legislature, twice in bids to sit in Parliament.

What is the opportunity visible ahead? I put the question to the trim prime minister with the ruggedly round face and quick-moving, expressive hands.

"Maneuverability in world affairs today is left largely to the medium-sized powers," he replied, choosing his words carefully. "Sometimes the big powers are too committed, too lined up. They cannot be flexible. We can.

"Canada thus can be a 'bridge' power—a bridge of conciliation in many directions. Between the United States and Britain, of course. Between big countries and the underdeveloped nations. And between West and East."

For instance, in the UN, Mr. Diefenbaker reasoned, Canada can express the viewpoint of the medium and small powers. It can make recommendations which will be heeded. On more than one occasion—the Suez crisis, for instance—its proposals have been adopted. At the time of Suez, Canada was an influence for moderation and for order—for getting the British and French troops out of Egypt, yes, but also for putting a UN force firmly on the Egypt-Israel boundary.

"Canada's counsels are persuasive, are accepted, because she is not regarded as having an ax to grind," the prime minister said. "Leaders of free Asia do not see Canada as motivated by anything but a desire to promote peace."

The preceding Liberal regime, with Lester Pearson its widely known foreign secretary, hewed to pretty much the same line—in fact, he was in power when the Suez crisis exploded. But around Ottawa one gets the impression that, whereas the Liberals spoke softly of their aims and whereas they soft-pedaled their Commonwealth operations, the new "Diefenbaker party" will do things much more emphatically. There will be no "British understatement," though the regime is strongly pro-British.

Other Canadian prime ministers have made Commonwealth tours in the course of office. But Mr. Diefenbaker is traveling early and traveling widely. He is getting to know Commonwealth leaders. His mind dwells much on the subject of Commonwealth talks, the Colombo Plan, Canada's contribution to Commonwealth development and investment. He early convened a finance ministers' conference of Commonwealth countries in Montreal.

I believe that Mr. Diefenbaker sees Canada's destiny particularly in terms of strong leadership within the Commonwealth, and as counselor and helper to its underdeveloped countries.

Canada, he pointed out, already has stepped up its contribution to the Colombo Plan from 25 million dollars to 37 million dollars, and intends to make it 50 million dollars annually. It has given 10 million dollars in credits to the fledgling West Indies Federation and is contemplating a "free-trade area" with that federation. It is planning development aid to Ghana. These are big steps for a country of Canada's population.

"Canada very frankly believes in the precept of being 'thy brother's keeper,' " the prime minister continued. "We simply have to help. We must see that economic standards are raised. To offer merely the blessings of parliamentary government—much as I admire Parliament—is not to fill empty stomachs."

There are those who argue that Canada here is thinking mainly about financing its export trade. These people miss Mr. Diefenbaker's sense of mission, the evangelistic zeal which enters his thinking. A sharp little question went the intimate rounds of official Ottawa recently. "Have you caught the vision yet?" The vision meant was that of Mr. Diefenbaker—a vigorous Canada with a strong world mission, including its Commonwealth role.

I think we shall see Mr. Diefenbaker, with his restless energy and need to accomplish, devoting much effort to making Canada's name and leadership known throughout the

Commonwealth. After years of what some said was "downplaying" the Commonwealth, this is eminently worth while. Britain constantly shies away from using the "hard sell" in Commonwealth affairs, afraid that this would be misunderstood as dictation. Canada can exert leadership without undue risk.

"The Commonwealth," declares Mr. Diefenbaker, "provides many tools for building better relations among peoples. It supplies economic assistance. It practices nondiscrimination. It inculcates understanding between many races and peoples."

Canada's clean-cut prime minister, a Baptist and a Mason who neither drinks nor smokes, thus speaks in terms of more than economic assistance. Canada is demonstrating a large degree of harmony among races. English and French have learned to live together. Since 1950, 1.3 million European immigrants have made Canada a new melting pot—Germans, Hungarians, Poles, Dutch.

"Our leadership against discrimination among races will be effective to the degree to which we practice nondiscrimination in Canada," Mr. Diefenbaker remarks.

Admittedly Canada does not permit West Indians to settle there, and various Asian members of the Commonwealth have voluntarily limited their immigration to Canada.

"I am of mixed origin myself," Mr. Diefenbaker says proudly. With a German name—because his great-great-grandfather hailed from Germany, though his mother is Scottish—he was early impelled to fight to transform Canada's biracialism into simple Canadianism. As a college student he denounced "hyphenated citizenship."

As a lawyer he defended war-uprooted Japanese in Canada. In Parliament he labored to lift the requirement that Canadians must register every ten years, according to their paternal national origin: "B" for British, "F" for French, "G" for German, and so on. He once ironically argued that Britain's King George would have had to put the letter "G" after his name in Canada because of his Hanoverian origin.

That regulation is now discarded, and since World War II Canadians have Canadian, not British, citizenship, thanks to his vigorous efforts. No wonder Mr. Diefenbaker is estimated to have received 90 per cent of the vote of non-English, non-French Canadians.

As we talked, clerks and secretaries came on duty, and there was a bustle in the reception room as emissaries of the Royal Society of Canada and the Geological Association of Canada formed up to present plans for further geological exploration of Canada's Arctic islands. Canada is laying intensive claim to the islands which reach right up to the North Pole, Moscow's objections notwithstanding. Mr. Diefenbaker has made a tour of Canada's colorful northland.

The prime minister's speech, some of his mannerisms, many of his ideas, are from the Canadian West. He was born in Ontario but his family moved to Saskatchewan when he was eight. Of the prairie he has remarked "your companionship becomes either the outdoors or books." Young John Diefenbaker read lots of biography as a boy (Lincoln and Gladstone were his favorites). He early determined that he was going to be a lawyer. At the University of Saskatchewan his college magazine predicted he would one day lead the opposition in Parliament.

"We lived in a new world out west," Mr. Diefenbaker recalls. "We saw the opening of the west, the arrival of the first major influx of immigration. We had settled around us people of various racial origins; we saw the beginning of that Canada which we have today."

This Canada of today is a "have" nation, he points out. It is rich in iron ore, natural gas, uranium, lead, zinc—a veritable storehouse of the free world. The United States is becoming a "have not" nation in some of these items.

Talk turned to Canada's relationship with the United States. "I am not anti-American," the prime minister declared. "I am, however, strongly pro-Canadian."

Canadians of all parties resent being "taken for granted" by the United States. John Diefenbaker has made sure, early, that he isn't going to be taken for granted by Washington.

Mr. Diefenbaker feels that the Ottawa visits of President Eisenhower have been very useful. Assurances were given against further disposal of United States farm surpluses abroad in ways that would injure Canada. There are plenty of unsettled problems: Washington's restrictions on imports of lead, zinc, and oil; the oversized American investment in Canada; the problem of sharing the waters of the Columbia River basin.

But relations are on a better footing now. One of the lasting results of the president's Ottawa trips is that relations have been put on a hearty, first-name basis. It is "Ike" and "John" now, when these two statesmen talk or write to each other. This keeps discussion friendly, builds understanding more easily.

A brilliant, cold day had banished the early shadows cast

on the broad lawn outside the windows by the Gothic spires of Parliament. That evening, a nation a-hustle would be flashing its neon signs of civilization across four thousand miles of territory where once only the Northern Lights winked down.

"Canada is entering the last half of the twentieth century in common dedication to achieving a great nationhood," Mr. Diefenbaker summed up. "We are now where the United States was when Calhoun and Webster saw the 'new day' of the American republic."

The "new day" perceived up north is a day fruitful with enterprise, with Canada's voice respected in the UN and in the Commonwealth, its foreign-aid program helping to bridge the gap between the highly fortunate and the newly emergent peoples, its statesmen traveling frequently and far.

Canada's role is also that of a defense partner of the United States and in NATO. In fact, the age of missiles has put Canada suddenly and directly on the firing line.

"We say up here," said Mr. Diefenbaker with a smile, "that 'between the U.S.S.R. and the U.S.A. is US.' It's very true.

"Perhaps that is why we are thinking in terms of rational trade with the Soviet Union and even with Communist China. This doesn't imply immediate recognition of Peking. But trade may help to bridge some of the impassable barriers when nothing else is effective."

Merely to govern provincially would not suit Prime Minister Diefenbaker. Canada is a dynamic, fast-growing nation. He notes the illustrious names of prime ministers who have preceded him. He wishes, I believe, to be numbered among the great, effective prime ministers.

In this era of friction and cold war, when the middle-sized

nations can accomplish so much by their councils of conciliation and their proffers of assistance with no strings attached, it is entirely fortunate that Canada is feeling these stirrings of maturity and that Canada's prime minister has potentialities for leadership.

Finale

PICK UP a newspaper in Asia, the Middle East, or Africa, and you won't have to reach beyond the front page to discover the hopes, the aspirations, the strivings of this planet's newly awakened peoples.

The Accra press reports an African hydroelectric power project. Jakarta tells of cementing closer relations between Indonesia and the new Malayan federation. Tokyo's *Asahi Shimbun* describes a "development" mission touring Southeast Asia. A Cairo newspaper speaks confidently about financing the Aswan Dam. India reports pooling of Western loans and credits to salvage its second five-year plan. And Chiang's "Little China" extends foreign aid to Viet Nam!

Everywhere capital development programs are springing up. Village improvement is swinging ahead. Prospects of receiving foreign aid from the United States—or West Germany—or the Soviet Union—are being assessed.

Meanwhile new premiers and new foreign ministers are a-traveling back and forth, making "good-will visits," discussing trade, broaching alliances.

A billion and a half people in Asia, Africa, and Latin America, too, are striving to assert their national identities, to move into the twentieth century, to improve laggard living standards.

This upheaval, this awakening, strikes any global traveler immediately. In summing up conclusions at the end of a selective tour of Asia, the Middle East, and Africa, this is one "constant" which leaps to notice everywhere. And even in Eastern Europe the Yugoslavs proudly boast about their industrial upsurge, Poland briskly announces that it is consuming more meat than West Germany, and the Soviet Union recounts a "year of glorious accomplishment"—meaning that seven new blast furnaces, fifty-seven coal mines, and various other new "capacities" in oil and chemicals were achieved in the last twelve months.

Some of the new countries have eyes marvelously bigger than their capacity to digest. They want steel mills when they should be wanting small-scale consumer goods factories. They talk of vast African federations when they haven't enough bilingualists to establish liaison with the country next door.

But they are not going to be denied. Nationalism is on the march. They have discovered—they think they see—what modern technology can accomplish. They usually feel the government should own the means of production, and they may have curious ideas about how to attract foreign private capital. But the depressed 80 per cent of mankind "wants in" with the prosperous 20 per cent of mankind.

The West should take careful note of what these "great expectations" portend. And of how Moscow is seeking to capture the undecided. The Congressional subcommittee which voted to cut the United States Development Loan Fund—loan, not gift—should take special heed.

This, then, is a dynamic fact of these times. There is a related factor which redoubles the dynamism of the awakening. That is the teeming upsurge in population all over Asia, Africa, the Middle East.

What, if anything, can be done about what happens when even a little sanitation and modernization begins to lower the mortality rate, while the birth rate continues to multiply humanity?

In Jakarta, capital of Indonesia, the Dutch—before their abrupt exit—built a broad street into the suburbs. It was intended to be lined with the neat factories of small industry—a kind of "green and garden" avenue. Today it is jammed along its entire length with shacks and rickety homes and hovels—the modest abode of thousands of people of teeming Java. Most of them are "squatters," moving in from the almost equally crowded countryside.

Regard this ribbon-development anthill, and you can visualize the population problem of Asia. You can picture the equally crowded Indian state of Kerala (where the Communists have won local elections), you can understand the worry of New Delhi where the Indian government now approves birth control, you can be appalled at Communist China's boastful disregard of the atomic bomb (because, Peking says, many hundred millions of Chinese would survive nuclear war).

In Washington the Population Reference Bureau has reported that the world's population increased by 90 million in the two years 1957–58. This is the same as adding a nation the size of France to the world every year. "The world has not begun to feed, house, clothe, and educate its present 2.8 billion people properly," warns the bureau.

What shall be done? Can mankind go on adding to its problems this way? India is not yet self-sufficient in foodstuffs despite two five-year plans, nearly completed. Indonesia has tried futilely to ship people from crowded Java to the outlying islands. Eventually, given higher living standards, the birth rate is supposed to subside. But it is on the increase even in the United States and Western Europe.

Population pressures are not insoluble. But, unsolved, they add faces to the city mob, they heat up the tensions, they make governments more frantic in their efforts to industrialize, to stay in power, to keep abreast of the tide.

This is why, one supposes, scholars like Germaine Tillion write that a little foreign aid can be more dangerous than none at all—for the modicum of aid may shrink the mortality rate while doing nothing much to help the country radically to boost its food production or expand its job-making industries.

So this is one more observation along the road of the quick traveler through the emergent countries. There are also less alarming discoveries.

One, for instance—and this is stated with great care: It appears that a dawn of alertness to the schemings of Communist Moscow and Peking is slowly breaking over free Asia.

The Soviet behavior in Hungary, Peking's launching of its barrackslike communes, the strident scheming of local Communists, the Moscow-supported drive against President Nasser's influence in Iraq and, finally, Red China's brutality against Tibet—all of these have chilled somewhat the warm regard which various presidents and prime ministers formerly had for the Soviet system.

India's Prime Minister Jawaharlal Nehru does not admire Communist China's behavior in Tibet or its encroachments in the other border, buffer states north of India. Burma is worried over its boundary disputes with Peking. Malaya has courageously shut down its mainland China bank and has banned the "dumping" of Chinese textiles in the federation. Indonesia resisted Moscow's effort to pose as an "Asian" nation at the recent Cairo conference of Asian countries. Yugoslavia's President Tito has been preaching nonalignment in his recent tour of Asian-Mideast countries.

This is not to say that New Delhi will spurn the Soviets when they come offering a new steel mill or cultural exchanges. Or that President Nasser will not continue his flexible neutrality, shopping on both sides of the street, accepting offers from East and West. But it does mean that the old days of uncritical admiration of the Soviet policy line are vanished. It is realized now that the bear has claws.

There is a dividend here, too: American policy now is viewed with a kindlier eye. And, of course, Washington has helped this along, not merely by foreign-aid programs but more essentially by a veering of policy in the past two years and by dispatching eastward a more alert band of diplomats and officials.

High State Department officials no longer proclaim that there is something immoral about nonalignment. The United States welcomes—and strives to assist—nations which maintain a sturdy, though uncommitted, independence. India receives a larger share of American aid. (And, incidentally, one of the handsomest American embassies anywhere is the new edifice in New Delhi.)

Burma has resumed doing business with Washington. Indonesian high officials will quietly admit that the United States Seventh Fleet protects their "freedom to be neutral." The SEATO (Southeast Asian Treaty Organization) countries are, of course, friendly allies. In North Africa the United States is Tunisian President Bourguiba's "protector" as he sternly lectures France on its behavior in Algeria. In West African Ghana, Washington has at least a two-year advantage on Moscow, which has yet to open an embassy in Accra.

My impression is that the United States foreign service personnel in these emergent countries is today better equipped, more aware of local sensibilities, more widely traveled in the local country, more able to speak the local language than was the case four and five years ago. There is now less likelihood of a fatuous ambassador of the type caricatured in *The Ugly American*.

Voice of America and other information officials abroad still wish, however, that someone in Washington could break out occasionally with a brave and bold speech, with stirring new ideas for coming to grips with dismal old stalemates, with concepts particularly worthy of America. Says one Middle East American:

"Our USIS job is like an automobile running with the clutch out until someone in Washington can enunciate ideals which people believe in. What can we offer the world? Is freedom enough? Is capitalism a sufficient creed? The Communists are always offering doctrines. I wish we could do much more."

So America and the West have a continuing challenge in these lands where there is a vast hunger for new ideas, new philosophies—for more books, even for more newspapers and magazines of good caliber.

This brings me to another quotation from an observant Westerner in Asia, a comment which indeed has great validity for today. This embassy official said:

"Wherever there is a strong, independent leader in these parts whose people believe in him, there the Communists really cannot win."

One of the world's great dramas today is ours for the watching—and the helping—if we will sympathetically observe the efforts of these leaders, in what we might call the underdeveloped areas of the earth, to keep marching in humanity's advance into the second half of the twentieth century and its vast opportunities.

It has been more than a privilege to meet with Messrs. Kishi, Chiang Kai-shek, Sukarno, Abdul Rahman, Nehru, U Nu, Nasser, Ben-Gurion, Bourguiba, Nkrumah, and the others. Though occasionally one encounters a leader who, one wishes, would show more vision, by and large these men are patriots according to their own lights, working long hours to advance the interests of their own countries.

Observe these various prime ministers and premiers at close range and, in almost every case, it will be noted that they have established a special "rapport" with their people or have a particular and endearing claim on the allegiance of the populace. That is, of course, how they achieved their eminence.

The West Africans cheer Dr. Nkrumah because of his rousing early preachments of independence, because of his personal spontaneity, and because he has been able to appeal to the commonest village African in building his political party. The Egyptians admire President Nasser because they think his shrewdness and his good fortune have defeated combinations and armadas (the Suez invasion) far more physically powerful than the United Arab Republic.

President Sukarno is able to speak to the inmost heart of the Indonesian people. U Nu held power for ten years in Burma because he was known to be incorruptible in a time of corruption and because, very nearly a Buddhist priest, he is regarded as a saintly man. In Malaya, Tengku Abdul Rahman is acclaimed as a sophisticated, even-tempered individual possessed of great wisdom. And in India Prime Minister Nehru wears worthily the mantle of Gandhi, than which there can be no higher Indian praise.

One could go on. In almost every case, the mere routine practice of parliamentary or democratic government would be insufficient. Emergent peoples are not yet ready for it: literacy is too low, prejudice too high, experience insufficient. As the Indonesian official commented, there has to be an X factor, an added ingredient, to make government function.

In some cases it is the popularity, the magnetism, of the leader. In others, it is the ramrod discipline of the army which has had to step in when weak civilian leaders were unable to cope with chronic graft and infighting. Much as Westerners may wish for a fine-functioning two-party democratic system in far-off Afrasiastan, it will not be achieved for many years.

As always, there remains the problem of communication—East to West, West to East. I am reminded of what that sardonic and delightful newspaper editor, Mohammed Hassanein Heikal, of Cairo's *Al-Ahram,* said to me in the course of his choice lecture on American shortcomings:

"What we want from you, more than foreign aid, is understanding—understanding of what we are trying to do. Surely you can give us that."

Very frequently Western newspapers have managed to report only the intrigues, the foreign adventuring, the mistakes of some of these leaders. Unreported is the wide grist of favorable news concerning development programs, opening of new schools and colleges, agricultural reform, village improvement, building of new factories. These people like to be understood, to have their achievements recorded, even as do we in the West.

I have dealt little, in this summing up, with the nations of Europe or the Soviet bloc, mainly because their case histories are better known. In the emergent 70 to 80 per cent of mankind things are going to be happening rather fast from here on, perhaps not always peacefully.

Ghana was the "model colony" of the Gold Coast back in 1948, wisely ruled from London. Then came Kwami Nkrumah, inflated prices, and a march of war veterans—and suddenly widespread rioting erupted. The colony never really quieted down thereafter until independence was granted. The same history could now befall some of the other "well-governed" colonies of African Africa.

It will be touch and go in many lands, whether any combination of cabinets, army men or parliaments can ride the storms attendant upon this awakening of the people. Often the West can help to channel the new forces, can help fend off the worst pressures of hunger, confusion, Communist intrigue, impatience, suspicion.

But the job goes forward. In Egypt, I believe the Aswan Dam will be built—with or without help from the West. Actually President Nasser has already begun the undertaking, and anyone who knows the hopes which have been channeled behind it would know it could not be dropped now.

This leads to a final observation. All through the world tour, the one comment common to all leaders of emergent countries was something like this: "We are for peace; we are against war. And that is because we have a great job to do, right here at home. We cannot spare funds for armaments; we have all we can do to keep our development program in motion."

To what conclusion does this add up? Very straightly and simply to this:

These peoples have no time for war!

To them, modern war was the luxury of an industrialized European continent which almost wrecked itself in conflict. And nuclear war is unthinkable. And it is not merely that atomic war is holocaustic but that all war is a waste of precious energy, an anachronism, a relic of the past which cannot fit into today's society, which has so much waiting business before it.

This is a fundamental message from emergent mankind. One trusts that Soviet Premier Nikita S. Khrushchev, who often pays heed to world opinion, is aware of it. One trusts that other "brinkmen" also are aware of it.

Perhaps this lesson should already have been apparent to all of us. But when one circles the globe and sees the patient Indian and his bullock cart, the Indonesian laboring in his small rice paddy, the Japanese at his cottage loom, the Tunisian in his unfertile field, the Ghanaian waiting for water at the village tank, the plodding Yugoslav peasant, one realizes how tremendous a job lies ahead on this unfinished planet of ours.